Principles of
Dressage

Principles of Dressage

Kurt Albrecht

Former Commander of the
Spanish Riding School of Vienna

J. A. Allen
London

British Library Cataloguing in Publication Data
A catalogue record for this book is available from the
British Library

ISBN 0-85131-569-0

First published in 1981 by Verlag ORAC, Vienna

Published in Great Britain by
J. A. Allen & Company Limited,
1, Lower Grosvenor Place, Buckingham Palace Road,
London, SW1W 0EL

Printed in Hong Kong by Dah Hua Printing Co. Ltd.
Typeset in Hong Kong by Setrite Typesetters Ltd.

Contents

The novice dressage rider should not expect praise; he should only constantly endeavour to link his movements to those of his horse. In the absence of unity of movement between horse and rider, neither knowledge nor strength can produce artistic horsemanship.

Introduction

There is little point in studying serious books on the subject of horsemanship if one thinks of riding purely as a sport or a physical exercise. The recommendations here and elsewhere will be of no interest to riders who consider that the art of horsemanship is merely the mechanical skill of controlling a horse. The literature on the subject of horsemanship spans many centuries, from the works of the Greek Xenophon to those of riding masters of the present time. The science of horsemanship has been transmitted from generation to generation largely by word of mouth, and only a few masters have felt the urge to commit to paper the fruit of their study and experience, but their writings have ensured that the knowledge of the fundamentals of horsemanship survives intact despite the passage of centuries.

In former times, friendly partnership between man and horse was of vital importance, whether for transport, for the dissemination of culture or for warfare. Horsemanship has had an important influence on the history of mankind and therefore on civilization, and remained for centuries an indispensable accomplishment. Nowadays (and for the foreseeable future), the horse is used primarily as an instrument of sport or for rambling at ease in the country, and there are many riders who, when they buy a horse, take his goodwill for granted. The art of training a horse to obey his rider cheerfully is the fruit of centuries of research but, since it has little relevance to the vital needs of modern existence, it is in danger of being lost for ever. This danger can be averted only if persons who are attracted to equitation appreciate sufficiently the value of good horsemanship and are willing to acquire the necessary knowledge and skill.

Studying horsemanship can give hours of worthwhile and pleasurable occupation – not only on horseback but also in an armchair with a good book on the subject. However, one must be prepared to explore the subject in depth rather than be satisfied with the acquisition of elementary and superficial knowledge. As with other sciences, the learning process can be extraordinarily mind-opening. I am not thinking of learning the essential elements of horsemanship by repetitive practise, but rather of the acquisition of a sort of knowledge that cannot be expressed by cast-iron formulae; that which allows one to view every reaction of each individual horse in an entirely new light, and leads to better comprehension of the horse's nature and mutual understanding between horse and man.

One does not need to be an exceptionally adept horseman to want to probe deeply into the subject of horsemanship. Every enthusiastic rider should consider every riding lesson an opportunity to develop a special relationship with his horse. However, to derive sufficient benefit from the study of the treasure trove of experience contained in the serious literature of horsemanship, one has to recognize the existence, on the one hand, of 'principles', which are invariably valid for every horse and every rider and, on the other hand, of 'methods', which are especially applicable to individual cases. Every living creature has a personality, influenced by a multiplicity of factors, and while principles are unchangeable, methods may have to be adapted to special conditions.

It is to emphasize this distinction that I have called this book *Principles of Dressage*. The title is intended to signify that I am not presenting new theories but rather expounding the wisdom of centuries, though in a form devoid of all the ballast that makes so many books indigestible. By offering only important guidelines, I hope to give help to those riders who have to work out their own way of discovering the joy of good horsemanship.

It is in vain that the reader will search for illustrations. I have deliberately excluded them because I know from experience that illustrations are often taken as models to which all must conform; the fact is ignored that no two humans can be exactly alike and enjoy the same advantages of conformation.

The reader who is prepared to devote enough time and effort to bolster his personal talent with knowledge of − and adherence to − the inviolate fundamentals will probably lay the best basis for a successful partnership with his horse. If he does not possess the 'ideal figure' depicted in illustrations, he must not despair; the best horsemen of all times have not always looked perfect models of elegance.

Reflections on the Art of Horsemanship

The art of horsemanship, as it is universally recognized and understood nowadays thanks to the embodiment of its most important principles in the rules of the F.E.I. (Federation Equestre Internationale), is founded on two elements: the *art* of translating the theoretical basis of horsemanship into practice, and the *science* of fashioning the body and mind of the horse in such a manner as to dispose the animal to put his energy willingly and entirely at the disposal of his master, so that both rider and horse can be physically and mentally united in performance.

In the art of horsemanship, the most favourable aptitudes of a horse can only be exploited if the rider possesses the requisite knowledge. Even a modest degree of equine proficiency can be produced only by a rider or trainer who has worked to acquire a good measure of creativeness and craftsmanship.

Craftsmanship has to be acquired by consistent work; the rider may be able to find a good teacher or he may have to work alone – which is much more difficult. In either case, one of the essential conditions of being able to apply theoretical knowledge to the practical task of educating a horse is the right attitude of mind. Without this, attainment of even modest achievement will always prove elusive.

In the course of his long history of service to mankind, the horse was first used as a draught animal. Riding was understood to be no more than the ability to remain seated on a horse's back. In some way or another, the rider communicated his intentions to the beast, but usually by forceful means that frequently defeated their purpose. However, over a long period of time, particularly intelligent men discovered, perhaps unsuspectingly, the 'laws' of horsemanship, and were rewarded by the horse's appreciation and his willingness to serve his master devotedly. (It must be made perfectly clear that the most astonishing displays of skill cannot be called feats of true horsemanship if the horse is forced to execute movements without any assistance from the burden that he is forced to carry.)

Actions on the part of the rider purporting to control the horse have traditionally been called 'aids'. Only too often, from the point of view of the horse, they are not aids at all, but very disturbing and puzzling sensations. In fact actions can justifiably be named aids only if they are in perfect accord with the natural movement of the horse. The appropriate response of the horse will then eventually become a reflex in which the mind of the animal does not have to participate; in fact the horse will not 'know' that he is obeying an order from above. Ideally, a spectator should get the impression that the rider only has to think for the horse to execute the required movement as of its own volition.

This complete unity of minds and bodies of rider and horse was essential in mounted combat, and historical accounts of battles in which cavalry was engaged frequently mention that the issue of a conflict was determined by the perfect oneness of every man and mount of the victorious army. However, it is difficult for us to imagine the necessity of oneness of horse and rider which was so vital for our ancestors. Its image has paled into oblivion as its necessity has disappeared, taking with it the general desire to achieve such a perfect state of unison.

Disregard of this sort of harmony, which is the mark of real horsemanship, does not generally seem to scandalize the spectators of modern equestrian sport. But for those few who continue to hold it in high regard, there is little enjoyment to be gained from watching so many rough and ready performances, despite remarkable successes mostly owing to the exceptional talent of the horses.

Few men confess to the deep-seated motives that attract them to horse riding, but when occasionally the most noble of beasts consents unexpectedly to subordinate his will completely to that of his by no means totally confident 'master', the experience can be so delightful as to cause at least a small transformation in the rider's outlook. There are many who will never experience those wonderful moments during the whole of their life in the saddle, and some who have enjoyed them occasionally but who lack the strength of character to show their secret longing to pursue horsemanship as an art well worth utmost dedication. Yet the greatest joy that riding can give is unsuspected by all those riders who do not feel a strong attraction towards academic horsemanship and have no desire to apply themselves seriously to its study.

However it is not sufficiently appreciated that artistic horsemanship is not the ability to make horses perform particularly difficult movements; it is purely the attainment of complete accord between rider and horse, and it is by the measure of this accord that every performance has to be judged. To put it differently, no matter the degree of difficulty of the movements that a horse is asked to execute, it is the gracefulness of a foal playing at pasture that must be sought.

Art in horsemanship depends entirely on the expertise of the rider and not on the stage of education of the horse. At every level of difficulty, what is really being demonstrated is the craftsmanship of the rider. In all arts, craftsmanship has to be the result of consistent effort. Even prodigies have had to work consistently to develop their natural talent into supreme artistry.

The true art of horsemanship is not, however, the province of prodigies. Certainly, there are many riders so richly gifted with 'feel' that results which most riders have to achieve by perseverant application do actually seem to fall into their lap. Also we can read about the extraordinary ability of certain horsemen of the past who could transform the most recalcitrant equines into perfectly docile mounts, but who could not explain how they did it. Nevertheless, the art of horsemanship is based not only on talent but also on work, and there is always hope of achievement for the less talented who are prepared to apply themselves consistently. The stages along the way will probably take them more time to complete, but the moments of real enjoyment will be no rarer or less delightful for them.

The first requirement of artistic horsemanship is the mastery of technique. All riders have to strive towards this end if they want to emerge from the ranks of armchair experts. Technical fluency is not the same thing as unthinking adoption of a stereotyped method. A technically fluent rider is one who is able to select the method most likely to succeed in overcoming the special difficulties of every horse he has to ride and train. The solid basis of all methods, however, has to be knowledge of the physical and psychological make up of horses; this has not changed much since man first had to find the right way of solving the problem of getting horses to serve his ends and to subordinate their wishes to his own.

Two important conditions are essential if man is to play the leading role in the horse-rider combination:

1) He needs to acquire insight into the mind of horses. The faculty of empathy is better developed in some riders than in others; nevertheless empathy is the essential psychological foundation for the physical aids.

2) He needs to learn thoroughly how to use the physical aids; these are based on Newton's laws of motion and are the rider's tools. Mastery of the aids is essential and a rider who does not know how to use them cannot ride a trained horse, let alone educate one himself.

These two conditions are as essential for the unambitious rider as for the dedicated one who aspires to attain the summits of achievement in horsemanship.

It is the feeling of unison, between himself and his horse, which constitutes, for the thinking rider, the deep pleasure of riding. On the contrary the rider who, from the outset, unsympathetically nags a horse to make him conform to a standard and measures his willingness by his unprotesting compliance with even unreasonable demands, utterly compromises the achievement of this state of unison.

The more favourable the disposition of a horse, the more prejudicial to his education is overimportance attached to some imperfections of conformation. Although there *are* some serious imperfections, there are others which are neither striking nor considerable weaknesses, but which have always been and will continue to be strongly disparaged in certain quarters. The essential requirement of 'purity of the gaits' can hardly be the reason for the excessive emphasis attached to perfect conformation.

Despite their imperfections of shape, many untamed 'unplanned' horses are much more attractive and graceful than perfectly proportioned 'robots' who have lost all charm and brilliance as result of human efforts to eradicate all imperfections of conformation.

The unbiased observer of horses deporting themselves at liberty in the paddock does not look for flaws of conformation, he simply enjoys the vision of a combination of power, beauty and elegance. But as soon as a saddle is laid on the horse's back, the miserable creature becomes the subject of carping criticism and is, in a certain sense, dismembered as each part of his anatomy is scrutinized and found to be defective.

The strictest standard of correctness of conformation and gait does not allow the animal to compensate for some weakness by showing other strong points. Man is only too ready to overlook his own imperfections but arrogates the right to weigh those of the horse with an apothecary's scales. Attractiveness, moreover, does not depend entirely on perfection of shape; small irregularities can make the animal more rather than less endearing, although more personal effort and knowledge on the part of the rider is certainly necessary to make up for what nature has not generously provided.

In the art of horsemanship, what kind of perfection are we looking for? Do we want a cold-blooded machine that conforms as closely as possible to precise canons of equine beauty but has been deprived of all traces of spirit, or a horse with a charming disposition even though we may have to accept that, in shape and proportions, the animal can be criticized on some minor points?

Those who prefer the latter may well seem misguided but their view should not simply be seen as opposed to present day notions; the trouble is that too few riders nowadays have enough knowledge to be able to interpret correctly the rules and regulations surrounding the art of horsemanship. If one believes that a horse is just some sort of instrument of sport, then it is understandable that all possible defects should be discovered before deciding on a purchase.

However, equestrian sport would certainly be better served if the rider's rather than the horse's deficiencies were put under the magnifying glass. It is known that there are riders who hamper a horse so much in his movement that, even if the horse has very considerable natural aptitude, he may give an impression of mediocrity. Even so, this is a fact that is rarely pointed out frankly by judges of dressage tests. The discomfort and humiliation that some horses have to endure is tactfully left unmentioned; judging of dressage is always harder on the horse than on the rider.

Defects of temperament cause much greater difficulties and they cannot be lightly dismissed. They may be manifested by irritability, inattentiveness, stable vices or a generally hostile attitude to humans which vents itself in biting and kicking. The influence of the environment in the establishment of behavioural disorders is widely acknowledged but it is too often overlooked that most vices develop in foalhood and persist after this. The famous capacity of horses to remember past events has advantages but also some very harmful consequences.

It is never wise to undertake the riding or training of horses with serious temperamental defects. They are seldom corrigible except by riders with far above average talent and expertise. The same applies to horses who have been turned sour by bad training. Their reschooling has always been considered a task to be undertaken only by exceptionally skilful trainers but, although they may behave when they find themselves in the hands of the expert, they are always quick to discover and exploit the slightest lack of skill in a less competent rider.

These notions formed the ABC of horsemanship that had to be learnt by all riders of former times. Then, however, horses and riders depended on each other for survival and, as the rider gained in experience, the right relationship would eventually be established. Such mutual dependency no longer exists and the worst that the rider can suffer nowadays is loss of face or money.

Of course, one should not overgeneralize; it would be untrue to say that all riders of our time think of horses as soulless machines, indeed, a considerable number of riders endeavour to establish a friendly rapport with their horse. Such endeavour should not be regarded as a rather irksome obligation; on the contrary, showing the horse some measure of affection and respect should be a pleasure.

The demands this makes on human physical and mental energies are not particularly onerous, provided the rider understands how to exploit the natural reactions of the horse instead of constantly opposing them, and that he always respects the important principles of horsemanship.

One of the most fundamental principles is that the rider must understand the physical and psychological make up of the horse, and the horse must understand the meaning of the rider's actions. If the rider is incapable of understanding the horse, the horse clearly cannot understand the rider either and may well misinterpret his indications completely.

Mutual understanding is the foundation of the education of horse and rider. The rider must have a sound knowledge of animal psychology; the horse must learn to accept the aids and to understand their meaning because the aids are the only means of communication from rider to horse in their partnership.

Too often it is the rider's inability, or refusal to appreciate the intellectual and physical limits of his horse that is the cause of ineffectiveness of the aids, of the horse's supposed unwillingness to obey and of the rider resorting unfairly to coercion and punishment.

Any rider who dismisses the necessity of psychological sense must sooner or later realize how much of his own strength he has dissipated in his efforts to gain his horse's acquiescence. *If one can see the world only through one's own eyes and is incapable of appreciating that it is perceived very differently through the eyes of the horse, one will inevitably be surprised by various of the latter's reactions. Furthermore, if a rider cannot correctly predict a horse's reaction to a strange event, his own reaction will always be tardy and often inappropriate.*

Many disagreements between man and mount are

the result of faulty diagnosis on the part of the rider, or of his misconceived efforts to fight the natural instincts of the horse instead of dealing with them intelligently. Even move crucial is the fact that *most of the cases of resistance or even of open rebellion by the horse to the rider's commands are founded on that most human of all human attributes, which is to forgive one's own weaknesses and to be intolerant of the weaknesses of others.*

We should reflect on the number of times in our life we have pushed our body to its limits, and it ought to shame us to realize that we take it as matter of course that the horse is so frequently asked to do just that. It is of course annoying when a human 'high' coincides with an equine 'low', but it is at such moments that the rider has to learn to behave like a true horseman.

Foremost amongst the qualities of a genuine horseman are modesty and consideration. He should be happy to climb off his throne sometimes to consult his equine partner. Too many riders think that they know the proper solution to every problem and will come up with a plausible explanation for every resistance. The mysteries of animal minds are admittedly difficult to unravel. There always have been riders with above average powers of feeling and understanding, and others only niggardly gifted in this respect. There are also perceptive riders who nevertheless lack the ability to make their intentions clear to the horse. The great horsemen of the past were undoubtedly outstandingly gifted, with exceptional ability to make themselves understood by their horses in order to make their own will prevail over that of the animal.

In the history of horsemanship, different methods

of training have co-existed or succeeded one another, but no method of training could have produced satisfactory results if riders had not possessed the faculty of understanding the horse and getting themselves understood by the horse. There certainly have been epochs when animal psychology was beyond the understanding of riders or when circumstances made it impossible to consider the feelings of the horse, but in such times horse riding was a primitive and violent exercise that certainly could not qualify as horsemanship. There have also been historical times when men of intelligence and sensitivity could apply themselves to the pursuit of artistic horsemanship with complete dedication without exposing themselves to accusations of eccentricity or effeteness.

Methods of training have, then, varied and the art of horsemanship has had its ups and downs. Nevertheless, the art has survived and will continue to survive provided that its principles are respected.

Riders who invariably resort to strong coercion may sometimes succeed in their aims. They will, however, always have to reckon with some secret antagonism which may not show while circumstances are unfavourable for the oppressed creature, but which will flare up at the slightest opportunity. In contrast, effective but considerate riders usually produce faithful equine servants.

Nevertheless, coercion *is* sometimes necessary. Horses are not always disposed to obey their rider's wishes with enthusiasm; in natural herd existence superior rank is not conceded without conflict. But in all cases of disagreement, the rider must be quick to feel the moment of the horse's surrender and instantly acknowledge it. Should he fail to do so, he will be unable to transform the moment of surrender into permanent willing acquiescence.

In the wild, very few cases have been observed of continuing humiliation of a defeated animal by its triumphant rival. In moments of victory, the rider also must be magnanimous, otherwise he can turn a conquered horse into a spiteful enemy.

The Aids — The Underlying Principles

Proper use of the aids is one of the most important principles of horsemanship. We do not know when and by whom the term 'aids' was introduced into the special vocabulary of the craft but it certainly must have had a godfather who coined it with intent. The idea contained in the term is that man must not seek to oppose the will of the horse but must instead help the horse to understand the intention of his rider.

There can be no doubt at all that the better developed the rider's ability to communicate his intentions to the horse, the greater are his chances of getting his will to prevail.

The word 'aids' as it is used in horsemanship is meaningful only if one understands that, to be effective, the aids must influence the mind of the horse as well as his body and limbs.

Mind and body are inseparable parts not only of reasoning man, but also of all living animals. We can only guess at the manner in which the controlling central nervous system of the animal analyses and organizes impulses, but we must at least realize that most animal activities involve active participation of the brain.

Opinions vary regarding the degree of intelligence of the horse, and scientific instruments for measuring it do not exist. We do know however that horses, though lacking the reasoning faculty of man, have the ability to make decisions and to associate effects and consequences. There are many instances when a rider has been reminded (often unpleasantly) by a reaction of his horse of some occurence buried so deeply in his own memory that he would otherwise hardly have recalled it.

The word 'aids' is generally understood to express the actions of the rider which produce reflex movements of the body and limbs of the horse by their effect on the lower central nervous system. We must not however overlook the importance of the psychological aids. These are all the influences of the rider on the higher nervous system situated in the brain of the horse, the command centre of the whole nervous system. It would be a grave mistake to believe that the two systems can be completely divorced or that it is possible at any time to act on one system separately from the other.

One of the most important principles regarding the use of the aids is that the horse must always be in the proper psychological conditions before any of the physical aids can produce its intended effect. The psychological aids come first. This is not recent knowledge but remains a principle which must be impressed strongly on all handlers of horses, especially trainers, riders or drivers.

For practical purposes, extensive knowledge and time-consuming study of equine psychology are quite unnecessary; in most cases a modest degree of knowledge of the subject is all that is needed. The important thing is awareness of, and respect for, the horse's mental and emotional make up. Such understanding will help the rider greatly to use the physical aids with discernment and to better effect.

The psychological aids encompass all impressions on the brain that are not stimulated by actual contact with the horse's body. First, it is necessary to remember that, despite centuries of domestication, the horse remains essentially a herd animal, even though nowadays he has to accept the company of man most of the time rather than of other creatures of his own species. It is because he is basically a member of a herd that he recognizes and respects rank. Struggling to establish superior status is an instinct that will never be completely eradicated; in the herd, ascendancy has to be established and then constantly defended. This fact has to be recognized and must always govern the relationship between man and horse. *In his dealings with horses, man must first establish his ascendancy and may subsequently have to reaffirm it with varying degrees of frequency.* A rider or trainer who willingly abdicates his position of authority on more than one occasion, or who is unable to preserve it whenever challenged by the horse, is soon in the estimation of the latter 'reduced to the ranks' and considered unworthy of respect.

One of the most important psychological aids is, therefore, firmness and fairness in all dealings with one's four-legged comrade; an attitude that never leaves room in the mind of the animal for any doubt about either the superiority of man or his trustworthiness. Acceptance by the horse of his inferior place in the social order is the best guarantee of a peaceful relationship between man and horse.

Yet legitimate authority must not turn into tyranny. Horses are intelligent enough to make the distinction; man also must have the intelligence to appreciate the difference. However, although every abuse of authority will provoke resistance, it has to be said that permissiveness has equally adverse consequences. The degrees of disrespect that it encourages can range from impishness and inattentiveness to downright disobedience; faults that are always difficult and often impossible to correct.

A horse who does not question the authority of

his rider is calm and in a favourable psychological state for satisfactory work. An agitated horse is always more or less uncooperative. The causes of agitation can be manifold but they are usually anxiety or fear inspired by disagreeable stimuli from the environment, by bodily pain or discomfort, or by unreasonable demands on the part of the rider.

If alarming external circumstances are the cause of the horse's agitation, the rider's most effective aid is his own imperturbability. This reinforces the horse's trust in the rider and helps him to overcome his fear.

Unreasonable demands are only too frequently the cause of a horse's excitement. The rider or trainer should always realize if he is overtaxing the horse's powers of understanding, but unfortunately his ambition too often drives him to overstep the mark. Curbing ambition is obviously the best aid for overcoming the horse's tenseness.

The expert horseman easily recognizes the first signs and root causes of mounting excitement and knows how to behave to calm the horse or at least how to avoid aggravating the nervousness. A rider who lacks feeling and understanding will not only react too late but will then usually react in the wrong manner. The wrong reaction or an untimely reaction will almost invariably provoke an increase of excessive tension.

Whether a horse's agitation is due to fear or perplexity, any aid, in the generally understood sense of the word as an action of seat, legs or hands, will increase the horse's excitement. The rider may, however, intentionally decide to liven the horse to prepare him for some special task — make him more 'mobile'. Knowledge and feeling are then essential to produce the required reaction.

Every rider and trainer must have the patience to study these simple but important facts of horse psychology.

Concern for a horse's physical or mental indisposition is another important psychological aid. One may be tempted to dismiss this as sentimental rubbish. Nobody denies that a human's performance is much affected by his psychological state, and that the psychological state is, in turn, probably conditioned by a physiological state. However, man arrogates to himself alone the right to have moods and is not usually disposed to grant it to animals — except as on occasional excuse for his own shortcomings. Nonetheless, a marked disparity of moods of horse and rider is not infrequent, and a rider's inability to control his own emotions will have a very unsettling effect on the horse.

Psychological aids, in contrast to physical aids, are not difficult to learn or to apply. They require on the part of man only the intelligence to appreciate that, together with the faculty of reason given to him, there must go a sense of responsibility for the mental poise of the animal in his charge. His repertoire of countermeasures has to be as complete as a horse's stock of reactions to external events. The reasonable rider, conscious of his position of responsibility, will take the little trouble required to study horse psychology and will thus prepare himself to meet any situation in the most appropriate manner.

Experience is obviously the best teacher, and if one is short of experience, one can avail oneself of the experience of others. There are plenty of good books in which past masters have recounted the incidents of their long involvement with horses and described their own reactions. These may not have been identical, but the reader should not feel confused; somewhere, at some time and somehow they must have met with success. The disparities only go to prove that there is no stereotyped method of educating horses, and that a method which may be appropriate with one horse may be totally inappropriate with another. One way or another, the superior brain of man, the thinking animal, must always carry the day.

Aid Applications

Control of the horse by the rider depends on the use of the seat, legs and reins. The influences of seat, legs and reins constitute the direct physical aids.

Direct physical aids are less complex than the psychological ones. Reins, legs and weight make up the ABC of equitation. There are other physical aids known as artificial aids, designed to offset in the rider's favour the mechanical disadvantage of relative lightness. It is useful to understand their principles but, in practice, their use frequently produces the opposite of the desired effect in the long run.

Regarding the artificial aids I must cite an ancient warning — although I know that there are many riders who will turn a deaf ear: artificial aids that do not involve direct bodily contact between rider and horse (and frequently exclude it altogether) can cause physical damage to the horse; the rider must understand and appreciate their effect. As a general rule they should be used only by extremely skilful and knowledgeable riders.

The artificial aids may temporarily spare the rider's forces but they rarely help to eradicate the horse's faults; on the contrary, they often have the reverse effect. A distinguished riding master of the last century rightly said that the greater the use of artificial aids, the smaller the progress. It is precisely because they lessen the work of the rider that they also reduce his appreciation of the cause of a difficulty and usually in consequence make it impossible for him to work out the appropriate remedy.

The most important principle governing the use of the aids is that an aid can be really effective only if it is supported by another working to the same effect. Another equally important principle, which does not contradict the previous one, is that *neither rein nor leg aids can compensate for a faulty distribution of the rider's weight.*

In the case of very modest performances these things are of relatively small importance. The horse can offset a faulty distribution of the rider's weight and his incorrect position by assuming a position that neutralizes the adverse effect of the rider on balance. But when correct position or incurvation is absolutely essential to the preservation of equilibrium, the correct seat and distribution of the rider's weight are of paramount importance. *A correct seat is not therefore the futile obsession of the pernickety riding instructor; it is an absolute necessity dictated by incontrovertible physical laws.* Contravention of these principles does not only set limits on progress; it can totally block the way to *any* progress.

Complete accord between horse and rider is what makes a performance enjoyable for rider and spectator alike, but it can exist only if the aids accord with the movement of the horse; the activity of the rider can then help the horse to execute required movements with ease. In contrast, discrepancy between the movements of the rider and the natural movement of the horse transforms the so-called aids into disturbing influences which irritate the horse and make him feel insecure.

THE SEAT: POSTURE AND WEIGHT EFFECTS

The seat is the most important aid of all. The weight aid is the greatest asset of the rider — provided he uses it correctly... It is the quality of a rider's seat that determines whether riding is horsemanship or merely the burdening of a horse with a cumbersome load which he has to transport as best he can.

Learning to sit correctly is undoubtedly the most difficult part of learning to ride, and there is absolutely no hope of success in any equestrian discipline if a rider does not first apply himself to the acquisition of a good seat. Everything that has been written on the subject of the seat can be thus summarized: *in all the gaits, whether he utilizes the full (or heavy) seat or the half (or light) seat, the rider must endeavour to maintain his own centre of gravity as close as possible to the centre of gravity of the horse.* In theory, it is a simple enough prescription; in fact, it is not as easy a feat as it seems. Yet every rider who allows himself to be convinced of the importance of a correct seat will strive to achieve it both by attention to his own posture and by schooling the horse towards self-carriage, and will eventually overcome the difficulty. Respect for this principle of weight distribution is a precondition of harmony of movement and intent between rider and horse, moreover it is the most important factor of a secure and effective seat.

Firmness and effectiveness of seat are not dependent on force of grip or tension of reins but entirely on a correctly balanced position of the rider. A correctly balanced posture is the indispensable foundation of a 'deep' seat; every rider should understand that establishing this posture is a paramount necessity, and a riding teacher who neglects to observe and correct the posture or state of balance of his pupil and skips this part of his education is acting irresponsibly.

Alignment of the centres of gravity of horse and rider is as much a principle of balance and security in the light or half seat as in the full or heavy seat; in the light seat the rider's upper body is balanced on thighs and stirrups while in the heavy seat it is balanced on the bony triangular base of the trunk. The reason why the heavy seat should be taught first is that a rider who has not established it will be incapable of educating any horse to even a basic standard.

The expression 'deep' or 'heavy' seat must not be misconstrued. It does not signify that the rider must glue himself to the saddle by pushing down. The common misconceptions of both the light and the heavy seat produce stiffness and improper distribution of the weight: either a 'fork' seat, with hollowed loin, in which contact between the seat bones and the saddle is lost, or its opposite, a 'chair' seat, with a round back, wherein contact of the fork with the saddle is lost.

The stability of the correct, properly balanced deep seat depends on the ability of the rider to maintain at all times an upright posture with the weight of his upper body resting on three points. This is easy enough at the walk but not always easy at the trot or canter. Nevertheless, a rider who completely loses contact between one of the three points of his base of support and the saddle through an unforeseen movement of the horse is in a precarious situation.

The three points of contact are at the junction of the two ischia (seat bones), the broad, fairly flat bones which form the posterior and lower border of the pelvis with, in front, the inferior process of the pubic bone (the fork). If the pelvis is tilted so that contact between fork and saddle is lost, the result is the 'chair' seat; in the opposite case, when only the fork is in contact with the saddle, the result is the 'fork' seat. Both are equally incorrect and have equally prejudicial effects on the stability of the rider and his influence on the horse.

Even when the rider uses a weight effect by shifting his weight towards either the posterior or anterior limits of this base of support, contact between any of the three points and the saddle must never be completely lost.

By putting rather more weight on one of the three points of support the rider can, to some extent, either cause the horse to step further forward with the hind leg which has to support extra weight or induce the horse to move in the direction of the more loaded side.

The upper part of the body of the rider, (head, neck, shoulders and chest) has to be properly balanced above the pelvis and the three points of support. Perfect alignment of each of these parts is an essential condition of stability; additionally it allows the rider to control with precision the shifts of his weight which constitute seat aids.

Although the main stabilizers of the body are the pelvis and the thoracic and cervical vertebrae, the head must also be included. Its position is a factor of considerable importance in the balance of the whole. Inattention to correct head carriage can totally or substantially deprive the rider of the possibility of influencing the horse's movement by 'engaging the seat bones', that is to say decreasing the pelvic tilt (Germans use the term 'kreuz', [sacrum]. The sacrum is the inflexible lower extremity of the vertebral column, excluding the coccyx. It is wedged between right and left hip bones and immoveably connected to them, and is therefore as much part of

Traversiren auf der Volte im weiten Kreise links.
Le Travers sur la Volte sur un cercle large à la gauche.
N.º 26.   J. E. R.

the back as of the pelvis). An unbalancing head carriage has to be compensated for by an adjustment of the whole of the vertebral column, including the pelvis, and this jeopardizes the rider's equilibrium and prevents effective use of all the aids.

Another frequent and very serious source of difficulty originates in the position of the shoulder girdle. A round back, with shoulder joints turned forwards is even more prejudicial to the stability and effectiveness of the seat than a faulty head carriage. It weakens the whole posture by totally preventing the correct vertical position of the pelvic three point contact and it impairs the activity of the muscles that stabilize the vertebral column and expand the chest.

The stiffening of the muscles of the shoulders and upper arms, the turning forwards of the shoulder joints and elbows are the consequences of stooping – which is usually an habitual fault of posture in all normal everyday activities. Stooping interferes with the proper connection of the arms to the chest; this connection is an essential element of the firmness of the seat at those moments when the horse makes a sudden unexpected movement that threatens the rider's balance. On such occasions, rounded shoulders and lifted upper arms will automatically draw the trunk forward and loosen the rider's adhesion to the saddle, thus rendering him practically defenceless.

Tension in the shoulder joints and muscles of the top of the upper arms lead to faulty tension of other parts of the rider's body and is transmitted to the body of the horse itself which, like a seismograph, registers the slightest fluctuations of the rider's poise.

A drooping head moves the centre of gravity

forward and renders the rider's position less stable. The laws of stability require a correct position of the head; the neck must be held up straight between squared shoulders.

If the arms are not allowed to fall loosely to the vertical from the shoulder joint, the elbows also are stiffened, precluding both sensitive contact with the horse's mouth, and effective resistance should he endeavour to escape control. Whenever the sensitive elastic contact with the mouth through relaxed arms and forearms has to be transformed into steely resistance, the arms have to be immoveably fixed to the chest, and the effectiveness of resistance depends entirely upon the firmness of the whole seat. An incorrect posture of the rider is the root cause of innumerable difficulties in controlling direction and also of faulty carriage of the horse.

When riding a young or partly-trained horse, the rider may adopt a light seat, not only to encourage the horse to swing his back, but also to maintain his own posture above the centre of gravity of a horse who is not yet in self-carriage. However, the essential condition of stability cannot be satisfied if the rider rounds his back. A stooping rider has no inherent stability and is incapable of linking his movements to those of the horse. When riding a correctly schooled horse who is in self-carriage, the line of gravity of the rider must drop from the centre of gravity of his head through the centre of gravity of his trunk as a whole and the three points of his base of support, and will be in line with the centre of gravity of the horse.

The ability to control and use his pelvic movements, and the effect of his posture on the biomechanics of the horse, are the rider's most potent assets. It is undeniable that a rider who knows how to use his seat has a greater chance of succeeding in schooling a horse than one who relies on the strength of his legs or, worse still, on the misconceived use of spurs. The most vigorous use of legs or spurs can never replace either partly or entirely the sensitive, intelligent use of the seat. Indeed, activity of legs and spurs in isolation from activity of the loins disrupts the fluency of the horse's movements and creates a striking picture of discord between rider and horse. (Squeezing or tapping lower legs can never be synchronous with the horse's movement; they can never therefore be 'aids' but constitute instead disturbing sensations that a horse will eventually learn to disregard.)

Even when the rider rises to the trot, he must do so on a vertical axis, so that the displacements of his centre of gravity remain in accord with the displacements of the centre of gravity of the horse.

Bad posture on horseback can also arise from a vague knowledge of anatomy or misunderstanding of certain conventional terms. There are many riders who mistakenly think that the sacrum is the coccyx. The German expression 'engaging the kreuz' (or bracing the small of the back as the term has been translated into English) does not mean sitting on one's tail bone, but simply reducing the normal forward inclination of the pelvis and the natural hollowing of the back at the waist, thus merely drawing the coccyx closer to the saddle. 'Disengaging the kreuz' is done by increasing the pelvic inclination and pulling up the ribs, thus putting more weight on the fork than the seat bones. However, these shifts of weight must be slight and the 'three point contact' must always be preserved. If contact with one of the three points is entirely lost, the rider cannot 'sit deep' and his position becomes insecure. A rider who sits correctly upright, with his upper arms hanging vertically from his squared shoulders will automatically have a deep seat and will be able to produce the required seat effects by minute changes of inclination in his pelvis.

Suppleness of loins also allows the rider to produce a lateral weight effect by loading one seat bone more than the other. He can thus induce the horse to support the increased weight on one side of his back by more engagement of the hindleg on the same side, or he can bring about a lateral movement. Again, this lateral shifting of the weight must not be exaggerated because it would then unbalance the horse and produce the opposite of the desired result; the lightened seat bone must not lose contact with the saddle, neither should the contact of the fork with the saddle be lost.

A correct position of the lower parts of the body requires that the muscles which connect the thighs with the pelvis be relaxed, that the thighs and knees lie flat on the saddle, and that the lower legs or shanks be allowed to be weighed down solely by the force of gravity. The prescribed depression of the heels should be slight, since it must not impair the elasticity of the knee and ankle joints.

Active tension of the muscles of thighs and buttocks reduces the amount of friction between the saddle and inner surface of the thighs which assists the rider in maintaining his balance. Absence of fat on the inner surface of thighs and lack of tension in the muscles are obviously advantageous, since a flat thigh constantly provides more points of friction than a fat or heavily muscled one. The knees must not grip the saddle because their grip stiffens the whole leg. Rather, they must preserve their relaxed contact with the saddle in all normal circumstances, but can always be ready to grip in emergencies. Habitual gripping lifts the knees up and reduces the area of contact between saddle and thigh. On the contrary a 'deep' knee position provides effective friction between thigh and saddle. It also allows the rider to modify the position of his lower leg according to circumstances without having to change significantly the position of his thighs.

Depressing the heels is all that is necessary to produce the only moderately increased pressures of the lower legs which suffice as impulsive leg aids with a properly educated horse. The impulses are in fact the automatic consequence of the movements of expansion and contraction of the ribcage of the horse. Contrary to the belief of many riders, strong compression of the horse's thorax with the lower legs, or tapping legs, have less stimulating effect than unforced maintenance of contact; they succeed only in dulling the horse's reflexes. Moreover, if the legs are used too far behind the girth, the effect on the horse can be the very opposite of impulsive and can even provoke disastrous consequences, such as running backwards and rearing.

A correct seat will always be more effective than an incorrect one. However although a truly elegant seat is likely to be correct, elegance is not a precondition of correctness, and artificial efforts to force a supposedly elegant posture will usually induce postural faults. The natural elegance of a rider depends considerably on his or her figure. It is a gift of the gods for which one may be thankful, but a perfect figure is not a precondition of successful performance in equestrian sports or of good results in training horses.

Once again, it must be stressed that neither the effects of legs or hands can compensate for the inadequacy of the seat. The potency of the seat (that is, of the weight effect) as an aid is due to the fact that it evokes from the horse instinctive reactions to physical laws; reins and legs can do no more than reinforce the weight effect and coordinate the working of the different parts of the mechanism of movement. The smoothness of the movement depends on proper coordination of all the aids.

The light or forward seat is as much a balanced seat as the heavy vertical seat. Although the rider has to rely mostly on the stirrups to maintain his crouching position, the forward seat must also conform to one of the most important principles of stability: alignment of the centres of gravity of all parts of the horse-rider system. If the rider is left behind or gets in front of the horse's centre of gravity, he unbalances the horse and forces him to make unpredictable movement; with most horses, a disturbance of mental as well as physical poise is the usual result.

Irregular movement and disconcerting temperamental explosions are less often manifestations of a horse's insubordination than they are reflexive reactions to the disturbing influence of an inappropriate movement of the rider. However, few riders are conscious of their sins; most would rather blame the horse for any unseating movement on his part.

The trust of a horse in his rider is largely dependent

upon the proper deportment of the rider. If his trust is continually undermined, the horse will behave in the manner which suits him best. This is why there are so many spoilt, disobedient, jumpy or lethargic horses. Extraordinary knowledge and feeling are always required to reschool a spoilt horse and teach him to behave himself.

All rides who aspire to educate horses to accept their ascendancy and inculcate in them a reasonable measure of obedience have to use the full, vertical seat. If they wish to resort later to the light seat for the purpose of a particular sport, the horse's obedience must have already been developed in the vertical seat, otherwise the rider will always have to rely for success on the horse's good humour on the day. In the vertical seat, however, the rider can utilize fully to his own advantage the mechanical principles of motion, and is in a better position to make his own will prevail over that of the horse.

There are evidently moments when horses can be so strongly perturbed by unusual external events that they will momentarily override their normal reactions to the laws of motion. But emotions of this kind are transitory, and the physical laws will hold sway again as soon as circumstances permit, provided that the rider knows how to exploit them. If the rider is unskilful, upsetting impressions may linger longer and longer in the equine mind and a return to calm will be decided by the horse rather than by the rider.

Methods of training based on a sentimental 'love of the horse' and indulgence overlook the absolute necessity of teaching the horse to obey. They are always futile even when, exceptionally, they do not have disastrous

40

consequences. By this, I do not mean that there is only one valid method of training. The 'classical' school prohibits all excessive and ridiculous demands, but it prescribes that the horse must be educated to accept unconditional subordination to the rider; every method must aim at getting the horse to realize that this subordination is the natural way of life. Nonetheless it is essential that the rider must be fair; an untrustworthy rider produces a suspicious horse.

For the purpose of inculcating the habit of obedience the vertical full seat cannot be replaced by any other aid.

Careful observation of old engravings depicting horses and riders must lead one to conclude that — disregarding the difference in proportions between horses of those times and the modern equine — massive stallions were controlled by riders whose lower legs were not in contact with the horse, who held the loose curb rein in one hand and either kept the other hand on the hip or used it to carry a switch. To our contemporary eye, the rider's legs seem stiff and ineffective but nevertheless the horse is always represented in the execution of one or another of the most difficult movements of the high school. *Those artistic portraits clearly meant to convey the impression that the horse completely trusts the rider and that obtaining calm and willing obedience was the prime ambition of the trainer*. However, they also show that this aim was achieved through the perfect coordination of seat and rein effects. We may conclude therefore, that *effectiveness depended not so much on the weight of the rider, but on the proper use of his weight*. The horses were so well attuned to the seat effects that any increase in pressure on a part of their back, even by a rider of moderate weight, would be sufficient to bring forth the intended reaction.

The body of the rider has to be an integral component of the total horse and rider mass. When in motion, a horse must constantly make adjustments in position and movement to keep his balance. This is difficult enough on straight lines, but on curves the difficulty is substantially increased. It is a mistake to believe that a four-legged animal is in easier control of his balance than a two-legged one. The four-legged animal is less prone to a sudden tumble when equilibrium is imperilled but, when he feels a dangerous disturbance of balance a horse has to make a quick movement, often unperceived by the rider, to guard against a fall.

Disturbance of equilibrium by incorrect distribution of the rider's weight may cause a horse either to throw his head up, turn his hindquarters out, put his weight on his outside shoulder, or assume some position that makes him virtually uncontrollable. In such instances, the rider compounds the horse's feeling of insecurity by attempting to correct the movement with certain effects of hands or legs which are worse than useless, as he himself is not at that moment in a position to use those aids appropriately. *To be an aid, the seat or weight effect of the rider must not only be correct; it also has to occur at the right moment.* Once the horse has recovered balance, the rider must be careful not to jeopardize this again by making an inappropriate movement.

The weight effect is based on the laws of gravity and it is on curves that it is especially important. In order to remain controllable on a curve, the long axis of the horse's body must conform to the curvature of the figure being ridden. Therefore, the thoracic muscles on the inside of the curve will have to shorten, those on the outside will have to stretch. Consequently the inside feet will have to be placed closer to one another in order better to support the weight of the horse and rider. Should the rider exaggerate the inward displacement of his own weight, the horse will be compelled by instinct to compensate for this by turning his hindquarters inward and moving outward with his shoulders. In the opposite instance an inadequate adjustment of the rider's seat intensifies centrifugal force and the horse is willy-nilly obliged to turn his hindquarters outward and move inward with his shoulders.

Almost all four-legged animals incurvate their dorsal spine more easily to one side than to the other. Various theories have been advanced to explain this unequal suppleness but none is entirely convincing. However, the reason does not really concern us. As riders, all that we need to know is that the more elastic side, that is the one that can be more easily elongated, is called the convex or hard side; the opposite side towards which the neck bends readily — is called the hollow or soft side. It is only because the horse yields reluctantly to the rein on the convex side that this is said to be the hard side. Many vexing difficulties of control stem from this peculiarity. Lateral suppleness has to be equalized as much as possible if the education of the horse is to progress beyond the most rudimentary stage.

The result of this more or less pronounced resistance to the indications of one rein is that the horse does not respect or accept sufficiently the indications of the rider's leg on the hollow side. In fact the difficulty is not really due to a particular stiffness of the thoracic or lumbar vertebrae but either to an unfavourable conformation of the mandible or the superior cervical vertebrae, or alternatively and more often (although this is not sufficiently appreciated) to the relative weakness of one hindlimb and its consequent insufficient engagement.

Resistance to lateral flexion of the poll is corrected principally by the hands but it has to be emphasized again that correct rein effects are only possible if the rider is sitting correctly. On the other hand, resistance to effective engagement of a hindleg and incurvation of the dorsal part of the spine can be overcome only through the combined aid of seat and legs. In order to comply with conditions of perfect manoeuvrability, *the horse will have to alter his habitual way of balancing himself and understandably will at first resent the feeling of awkwardness this causes.* After some time the new way of going will inconvenience the animal less and eventually it should feel quite natural.

To return to the subject of the seat; apart from being 'deep', it must also be:

Supple. Excessive muscular tension of any part of the body, from neck to toe, is not only detrimental to the firmness and effectiveness of the seat, but also has a worrying effect on the horse.

Firm. The loin is the link between the upper body (head/neck/shoulder/chest) and the lower body (pelvis and thighs). Stiffness is certainly undesirable; nevertheless an elastic tension of back and abdominal muscles permits the quick reflexes necessary to preserve balance when the horse makes a sudden unexpected movement, while allowing arms and legs to remain in their proper position.

It should be constantly borne in mind that the slightest wrong position or movement of head, shoulders and arms, pelvis, thighs and lower legs is felt by the horse as a complete displacement of weight and affects his equilibrium.

A rider who wishes to improve his seat and is determined to work towards this end must understand the mechanics of movement of the horse and appreciate the influence of his posture; on the other hand, a riding teacher who just admonishes the rider for loss of correct posture without explaining the correlation between posture and reactions of the horse does not honourably fulfil his obligations.

Yet it is a regrettable fact that, despite the most serious studies and the most assiduous practise of riding, the number of riders who succeed in acquiring the kind of seat that amounts to virtual amalgamation of equine and human bodies is infinitesimal. More usually the mechanical effect of the rider on the movement of the horse is unfavourable instead of helpful. *Awareness of this fact is no reason for giving up riding. It is known that horses will put up with the inconvenience of carrying quite heavy loads provided that the load does not dangerously unbalance them; the horse will always, however, generously reward the rider who makes the effort to harmonize his movements.*

A truly elegant seat is nearly always a correct one, but this does not signify that an imperfectly proportioned rider does not have a correct seat. As I have said before, beauty and gracefulness depend on certain aesthetically pleasing nature-given proportions. If one has not been so blessed, it will always be difficult to be a perfect model of elegance on horseback and one will have to compensate for physical disadvantages by other qualities and to work harder to achieve the results which seem to fall in the lap of the fortunate few. Many of the greatest riders of the past certainly did not have admirable figures but, despite this handicap, they achieved supreme mastery of the art of horsemanship.

It should also be noted that horses reciprocally have a strong influence on the seat of the rider. A rider who for many years has ridden only one horse will suddenly experience all sorts of surprises when he starts to ride a different one. No opportunity to ride an unknown horse should therefore be turned down; it is always a revealing test of the adequacy of one's seat.

If the picture of a rider sitting correctly is firmly engraved in one's mind, one will be constantly reminded of the important criteria of correctness. They can be expressed as follows:

The seat will be the more secure the better the posture of the rider; the better he relaxes his thighs and buttocks to let his three points of support come into direct contact with the saddle, and the better the seat of the rider, the easier it is for the horse to accommodate the weight of the person enthroned in the saddle (instead of perched *above* the horse's back as is too often the case). A forward inclination of the head and neck, a round back and a crooked spinal column (the two go together), protruding shoulder blades and turned out elbows, stiffened arms and tucked-in abdomen are all enemies of the deep and correctly vertical seat.

The rider who succeeds in relaxing the tension of his muscles in contact with the saddle has a broad base of support, a condition of efficient balance. The better the three points of support formed by pubic and ischial bones remain in contact with the saddle, the better the horse will respond to the slightest alteration of their pressure on his back.

Relaxed thighs, hanging loosely from the hip joints and providing efficient friction with the saddle by their weight alone contribute to the stability provided by the contact of the three points of the base of support with the saddle. Any degree of active gripping, of contraction of the inner muscles of the thighs, is automatically transmitted to the buttock muscles and reduces the breadth of the base of support; strength of grip elevates the rider's centre of gravity and defeats its purpose — it makes him less rather than more secure.

The prescribed position of the knee does not imply its rigid adhesion to the saddle. The purpose of this prescription is to prevent gripping with the calves although, of course, it also enables the rider to secure his seat instantly in critical moments.

In equestrian parlance, the precise meaning of 'leg' is shank — the part of the leg below the knee. The shanks have to give the impulses that elicit the engagement of the hindlegs which is of fundamental importance for control of the horse from a seated position. They should never grip the sides of the horse forcibly and insensitively; their stimulating action is due to the alternating, rhythmical movements of expansion and contraction of the ribcage of the horse which accompany the movements of the hindlimbs. If the rider's thighs and legs are properly relaxed, the legs can maintain their contact with the horse's sides effortlessly, and the stimulating impulses are then automatically derived from the movement of the horse.

The rider does not produce such impulses with

his heels; however if the leg muscles are relaxed, an unforced lowering of the heel of one leg produces a pressure on the stirrup that can substantially reinforce the effect of the seat. Another result of the soft lowering of the heel is to tauten the calf muscles somewhat, thus enhancing the impulsive effect of the leg. This manner of tautening the calf muscles must not be confused with the totally detrimental lifting of the leg that is the result of trying to use muscular force to 'squeeze' obedience out of the horse.

If the ability to use the legs in the manner described is combined with a correct and therefore effective seat, we get the picture of a rider *allowing the weight of his trunk to drop without hindrance on its bony base of support; of a rider sitting easily upright with a supple waist which minimizes the transmission of the pelvic movements to the upper parts of the body. It is the stillness of the upper body which reduces as much as possible the disturbing effect on the horse's equilibrium of transporting a load with a centre of gravity situated so much above his own. It is this stillness also that allows rider and horse to 'go' together in perfect harmony*.

Changes in the tilt of the rider's pelvis, that is, the engaging or disengaging of the seat bones, cause the horse to feel more or less pressure of the seat bones on his back. However, these changes of pelvic tilt ought not to affect the vertical position of the parts of the body above the loin. The effect of leaning backwards stiffly goes far beyond the useful effect of 'engaging' the seat bones and very often provokes the horse to run away from the rider. A sudden forward inclination of the upper body will also abruptly impair the flow of the movement and produce irregularity of the gait. Both faults will agitate the horse.

It is not sufficiently realized that a faulty or un-steady head position of the rider has a considerably unfavourable effect on the horse's equilibrium. Erratic movements of the rider's head amount to constant changes of balance.

The best way to acquire a good, workmanlike seat in all the gaits and in all situations is to curb one's ambition, to avoid making demands upon the horse for which he is not ready, and to remember that relaxed legs and correctness of posture are the key to effectiveness.

The 'open' seat described above, in which the rider allows his weight to fall on the broadest possible base of support by letting his gripping muscles relax completely, is the best guarantee of preserving stability of posture and thus attaining effectiveness. On the contrary, riders with insufficient modesty and immoderate ambition will waste more time, and experience greater difficulty, in acquiring this deep, unconstrained seat.

To conclude this chapter, here are some additional details which can either assist or hinder the acquisition of an effective seat.

Since the criteria of a correct seat are the same as the criteria of good posture in general, being constantly attentive to one's bearing when standing or walking is excellent training. A correct vertical posture of the head and trunk on horseback is not a special posture applicable only to riding.

Besides this, in the early stages of training it is frequently necessary to have the courage to inhibit instinctive reactions to the behaviour of the horse which involve the loss of one, two or three of the points of the base of support. A rider who succeeds in overriding his primitive reflexes will also succeed in keeping the three points of his base of support (both seat bones and the fork) in contact with the saddle in the most critical situations. He will have learnt to master his equilibrium.

The seat can be said to be *accomplished* when a rider has discovered how to be so completely at one with his horse that the latter responds to all seat effects as of his own volition.

A *correct seat* enables the rider to impose upon the horse compliance, obedience and correct gaits without ever making more than moderate demands on his own muscular forces or those of his horse.

A seat is *unconstrained, easy and relaxed* when the rider sits still; in fact sitting still really means moving with the horse — neither more nor less — at the same rhythm as the horse. A correct seat must convey the impression that the rider is being passively carried along by the horse. Being carried along does not of course mean hanging on to the reins.

A seat is *firm* when the rider's bearing never deteriorates as a consequence of the horse's sometimes unpredictable movements, when he never collapses forwards, backwards or sideways and maintains perfect poise even when the horse moves irregularly.

The correct seat is *dynamic and elastic*. These are the qualities that give the rider 'feel' — the sensitive coordination of seat and hand actions which enable him to sense an impending change in the horse's movement and to accept it or prevent it.

The antithesis of a correct seat is a wooden, inanimate posture that has as unfavourable an effect on the horse's movement as inert luggage.

The following common faults will always be the enemies of a correct seat:

The drooping head and the stoop are the signs or the

cause of a defective base of support; they cause a forward displacement of the rider's weight on to his fork (and onto the forehand of the horse) and deprive him of the effective use of his seat. The fault is often asociated with a wrong position of the legs, either stiffly thrust forward or stiffly held backward.

Leaning backwards, with the trunk supported only by the two points of contact formed by the seat bones. The rider is behind the movement and very often in this manner involuntarily urges the horse to make greater speed, which he then tries to restrain with exaggerated use of the reins. Leaning backwards puts the horse on the forehand because it causes the propelling function of the hindlimbs to grossly predominate over their supporting function.

An incorrect displacement of the three points of the base of the seat out of the centre of the saddle; this necessarily entails deterioration of the upper body carriage.

In former times, the seat demonstrated the level of horsemanship of a nation, and judgment of the level of horsemanship implied judgment of the seat. As regards the future, the state of the art of horsemanship will depend on the importance attached by dressage judges to the seat and influence of the rider. Disregard of this essential element of horsemanship would lead to a serious decline of the art.

THE REIN EFFECTS

In the description of the various direct physical aids it is usual to start with an explanation of the rein effects, probably for the reason that they are the first with which the horse becomes acquainted. Apart from the voice, they are the first means of communication available to the rider and trainer. They are also fairly easily understood by the horse and usually accepted without resistance.

These rein aids are brought about by the pressure of the snaffle (bridoon) or the curb bit on the bars of the horse's mouth, or by pressure on the nasal bone when a lungeing cavesson or a noseband operating on the same principle is employed.

Nowadays the cavesson is usually resorted to only for work in hand, for leading the horse or for working on the lunge. We need not further discuss its use and we will concentrate our attention on those bits which are exclusively allowed by the F.E.I. in riding and driving competitions.

The effects of the snaffle (bridoon) and of the curb bit are quite different. Nowadays, on principle, it is with a snaffle that a horse is bitted in the first stages of his education. The main characteristic of the snaffle used to be, and continues to be, the jointed mouthpiece, but in some cases an unjointed mouthpiece working on the same principle as the jointed mouthpiece is used.

By virtue of its joint, the snaffle exerts a unilateral pressure on the mandible that causes the horse to turn his head in the direction of the pressure and to follow with his body the direction imparted to his head. However it is only in the earliest stages of training that one employs this simplistic effect for it does deprive the rider of a considerable part of the control made available to him by the use of a jointed mouthpiece.

As soon as possible, the horse must be accustomed to the other effects of the reins. One of the most important of these is the development of suppleness of the joints of the poll in vertical and horizontal directions, that is to say, flexion and inflexion. This already implies a certain coordination with the other physical aids.

The development of this suppleness of the poll — which must exclude absolutely the infliction of discomfort or pain — is nowadays recognized as being of great advantage in all equestrion sports, but this has not always been the case. In the past it was considered to be necessary only for what used to be called 'School' riding and is now known as specialized dressage riding. A considerable majority of riders were content (and are still content) to ride horses moving with stiff backs and stiff hocks because they had (or have) never experienced the pleasure of being mounted on pliant and therefore genuinely submissive horses.

As soon as the horse has learnt to accept the simple directional effect of the snaffle, the rider must teach him to respond to more sophisticated rein effects. *The most important function of the latter is to make the horse attentive to the next demand of the rider and to assist him (although mostly in a psychological sense) in carrying out the rider's instruction to the best of his ability.*

The effects of the reins, as of the other physical aids, are based on the scientific principles of motion but very little science or thinking is required of the rider if his horse has more good points of con-formation than weak ones, an especially good sense of balance, and the intelligence to make the correct adjustments to his equilibrium despite the erratic movements of his rider.

Unfortunately such horses are rare; most of us will have to compensate for the disadvantages of our mount in one respect or the other by understanding and thoughtful application of those laws of motion. To start with, we must understand the effects of the snaffle. By virtue of its jointed construction and its unilateral effect, it is much better designed than the curb (which has a substantially different function) for improving lateral suppleness or correcting unequal lateral suppleness.

For these purposes, rather than for the elementary one in the earliest stages of indicating changes of direction, the tension of the inside rein has to be matched by equal tension on the other rein. To put it differently, tension on both reins is always necessary, although each rein has to be used in a somewhat different manner and one rein comes into action a fraction of a moment before the other.

One would think that the use of the reins in turns or on the curves of the track (for example, when riding the corners of the manege), is simplicity itself and requires little explanation but, in reality, it is obvious that many horses are forced to compensate for the unbalancing effect of the rider's rein effects by assuming a position wherein they cannot maintain the regularity of the gait and which deprives the rider of effective control.

In order to preserve his equilibrium in turns, and on curved tracks to which he has to adjust the incurvature of his body, the horse must shift a certain proportion of weight onto his inside limbs. However, the rider's own weight must also be taken into account. This causes problems for the horse which we can easily appreciate by running with a heavy child astride our shoulders. In fact the horse must learn to execute this trans-ference of weight before he incurvates his body according to the curvature of the course rather than

Ballotade auf der Volte rechts.
La Balotade sur la Volte.
Nº 40.

J. E. R.

at the very moment of the change of bend. The change in equilibrium must precede the change of course. Therefore, the first requirement is that *the indication of the rider's intention by means of the reins must be given at a moment that gives the horse enough time to displace his weight and safeguard his equilibrium.*

An attempt to change the incurvation by means of the reins at the precise moment when the horse is establishing his new equilibrium has an unbalancing effect on the horse which he has to neutralize by counteracting. The countermeasures that he resorts to can be in the form of 'wrong bend' or counter-position, turning in of the hindquarters, thrusting against the inside rein or quickening the steps, and are nearly always accompanied by a loss of calm. If the rider continually acts with the reins in an incorrect manner, these defensive reactions of the horse become established and habitual. It explains why so many horses constantly execute changes of direction with a wrong position of head and neck...

A wrong bend provoked by untimely use of the reins cannot be corrected by renewed or stronger use of the reins. The incontrovertible laws of equilibrium force the horse to resist or disregard the rider's attempts to impose a correct head and neck position. Obedience would inevitably cause him to stumble.

It is not only the mistimed use of the reins which provokes the horse to resistance but also the degree of bending demanded by the rider. The belief that it is pre-eminently the function of the inside rein to prescribe inflexion and that the tension on the inside rein must therefore be stronger than on the outside rein (in order to produce more inflexion and consequently a tighter turn or a smaller circle) is a very common mistake based on a false assumption.

It should be clearly understood that it is the incurvation of the dorsal area of the spine that enables the horse to neutralize the effects of centrifugal force, and the amount of bending possible in this region is limited by the restricted possibility of compression of the ribs. Should the inflexion imposed on the head and neck exceed the possibility of incurvation of the body as a whole, the horse will be obliged to support on his outside shoulder the mass forced outward by centrifugal force, and the hindquarters will have to track beside the circular track. It is not unusual to see a rider franctically and unsuccessfully attempting to steer his horse and keep on a circular track by bending the horse's neck until his nose touches the toe of the rider's boot.

Thus we come at last to a discussion of the use of the outside rein. It has extraordinarily important functions and it is regrettable that this is not usually stressed sufficiently strongly.

One of these functions is to determine, in conjunction with the inside rein, the amount of inflexion of the head and neck. It is undeniable that the average degree of incurvation of the body depends on the degree of lateral flexibility of the dorsal section of the trunk; the incurvation of this region entails some displacement of the centre of gravity to the inside and consequently a greater proportion of the weight has to be supported by the inside limbs. One of the principal aims of the gymnastic training of the horse is to develop the elasticity of the back muscles and the lateral suppleness of the trunk. The incurvation of the body as a whole must be as uniform as possible, and extend from the poll, through the neck and ribs to the dock.

It is the outside rein that has to prevent the localization of the bending in the all-too-flexible neck, for a break in the outline of the neck can never be tolerated; but besides exerting this control on the neck, the outside rein must also fix the outside shoulder and frustrate all attempts by the horse to move his shoulders outside the circumference of the prescribed track.

The use of the outside rein is subject to the same rule that must govern the use of the inside rein; *the horse must always be given enough time to execute the change of bend and the change of equilibrium that goes with it.* Both reins must, therefore, be used in turns and on curved tracks: the inside one must warn the horse in good time of the rider's intention and must henceforth remain as passively in contact as possible while the outside rein, having first allowed the change of position, must then limit the bending of the neck; besides this, the resulting relatively greater tension of the outside rein represents a certain balancing aid for the horse. This does not of course imply a rigid tension of this rein but an elastic one, aptly described by one of the great masters of the past as the 'breathing outside hand of the rider'.

It is an important principle that *once the horse has established the new equilibrium involved in the change of bend and direction, he should not be disturbed by any further manipulation of the reins while he remains on the same course*; the rider must therefore restrict his aids to the use of the seat.

The outside rein also has a *collecting function*, for example when the horse has to gather himself to start or maintain the canter. If the outside rein is used on a straight course – when it is not being employed for the purpose of correcting a faulty inflexion — it restrains the outside shoulder for a moment, freeing the inside shoulder and inducing the horse to spring into canter. (When the canter is established, the use of the outside rein at the rhythm of the canter maintains the gait.) This gathering effect of the outside rein (half-halt), compacting for a moment the corresponding side of the horse's body, 'compressing the springs', is the key to more advanced dressage. It is an absolutely essential element of the education of a horse intended for that discipline. *The unobtrusive check with the outside rein (a merely warning kind of half-halt which in Germanic countries has preserved the French name 'Arret') together with the appropriate seat aid obviates the need for inordinate use of legs and in a sense helps the horse to educate himself, preparing him for the execution of the most difficult dressage movements wherein the rider's aids should be practically invisible.*

It is the jointed construction of the snaffle that allows pressure to be applied temporarily to one side of the mouth only, thereby influencing the movement of the corresponding hindleg. This distinct effect is not possible with a curb bit; the curb can only act on both bars simultaneously and, although this peculiarity of the curb allows more precise control of the rhythm of the gait, it requires perforce greater sensitivity on the part of the rider, who should not resort to it before he has acquired a correct and effective seat and understanding of his rein effects when the horse is bitted in a snaffle.

As regards the horse, it must be stressed that the curb is totally unsuited for correcting lateral stiffness and resistance to inflexion: the snaffle (bridoon) only should be used for this purpose. If any degree of difficulty in obtaining inflexion exists, it is still with his weight aid that the rider must give the first indication for a change of direction or a small circle; the reins are then used to allow the change of inflexion.

At this stage, if the horse is ridden in a double bridle, it is essential to adopt the three to one manner of holding the reins: bridoon rein only in the inside hand, both curb reins in the outside hand together with the other bridoon rein. This ensures that the rider does not apply more tension on one curb rein than on the other, a very prevailing instinctive reaction that is difficult to correct.

There are other important rules governing the use of the reins either to eliminate a particular resistance to direct flexion of the poll or lateral stiffness, or to obtain elevation of the neck and compliant bridling. It should also be noted that the reins are not employed quite in the same manner in two-track movements and in movements on a single track.

In the very first stages of training, the horse should be allowed to carry his head in the position which he finds most comfortable. This gives the rider a useful indication of the difficulties he may have to contend with. Although the horse has, in time, to be taught to carry his head in a correct position, it is from the natural position that corrections proceed and it should be evident that the correct position cannot be identical for all horses. Nevertheless, *there is an average correct position, in which the corners of the mouth are approximately level with the hip joints.* Pronounced deviations from this correct position, in one direction or the other (above or below it) indicate faults or weaknesses of conformation. This correct average head position must be preserved whether the rider is driving the horse to the bit to compact his frame or is yielding with the hands to allow him to extend his frame and lengthen his strides.

School movements designed to improve bilateral suppleness should not be practised before the horse has learnt to carry his head steadily in a correct position without constant intervention by the rider.

In practising flexions to loosen the poll at halt, the outside rein must give exactly to the same extent as the inside rein takes and it is of the utmost importance to avoid producing a break at any part of the outline of the neck. The horse must simply follow the indications of the rein, as if he wanted to look backwards without tilting his poll or bending his neck.

Resistance to lateral flexion or a tilting of the head are nearly always indications of some stiffness of the coupling of head and neck or of discomfort produced by compression of the parotid glands by a mandible of less than ideal shape. These difficulties can be eliminated in most cases by patience and the perseverance with systematic exercises; in any case the eradication of this localized stiffness is essential for otherwise it will remain impossible to establish a steady tension of reins and equal bilateral pliancy of the poll.

'Bridling' and 'elevation' of the neck cannot be achieved before the poll has become equally flexible bilaterally. The degree of rein tension on either side depends entirely on the horse's bilateral suppleness. Excessive 'softness' or yielding to one rein can be as objectionable as excessive 'hardness' or resistance to the bending effect of the other rein. *Developing bilateral suppleness without provoking the horse's temper requires in all situations great understanding and feeling on the part of the rider.*

The bending effects of the reins must extend to the hindlimbs of the horse and this condition can be satisfied only if there is no resistance to inflexion either in the neck or at the poll.

Once the pliancy of the poll has been obtained and the disadvantages of a rather narrow space between the branches of the mandible or an unfavourable conformation of the first cervical vertebra have been neutralized, the reins can then be used for three further purposes:

1) To remind the horse that he must maintain at all times a correct head position.
2) To indicate changes of direction and support the effects of seat and legs in two-track movements.
3) To warn the horse of a change of gait that requires collection.

The rein effects for these purposes become increasingly discreet as bilateral suppleness improves. *In ideal conditions, communication between the horse's mouth and the rider's hand can be so refined as to require no more than a closing of the ring finger of the rider on the curb rein to obtain the horse's compliance.* However, if one tried to define a precise degree of rein tension for each gait or exercise, one would give the wrong impression that it is invariable and that its effect is automatic. This is not the case; it all depends on the degree of submissiveness which has been achieved.

Nevertheless, one thing that has to be made clear is that – with an infinitesimal number of exceptions –

rein tension must never be so strong as to lead to an outright battle of wills between rider and horse. Violent rein effects are never pleasant for the horse and can cause considerable pain, but the horse is stronger than the rider and is always able to defend himself successfully against unreasonable restraint by the reins. *The best way of preventing the horse from using the enormous power of his neck and jaw muscles to 'play with the rider' and wrench the reins out of his hand is to gain his trust in the hand and to use all the aids in rational combination to obtain instinctive obedience.* The 'breathing hand' which repeatedly takes and immediately thereafter gives deprives the horse of the possibility of leaning on the rein to preserve his balance, and teaches him to remain in self-balance when this constantly changing pressure on the bars ceases.

Every rider and trainer ought to feel morally obliged to appreciate the effect of the curb on the bars of the horse's mouth. The higher the port or tongue groove, the harsher the pressure that can be exerted directly on the bars; the difference in length between the lower and upper cheeks of the bit determines the potency of the lever. Finally, one must not forget the enormous effect of the adjustment of the curb chain. The curb is a powerful mechanism which can give very precise control when it is used for its proper purpose; it can also easily turn into an instrument of torture.

The transition from simple bitting in a snaffle to double bitting is critical. If fear of the curb causes the horse to lose confidence in the rider's hand, the progress of training will be at least interrupted and in some cases may be seriously reversed.

The curb always applies pressure to both bars of the mouth simultaneously, even when a one-sided effect is intended. Shortening the inside rein will certainly induce a submissive horse to turn his head in the desired direction by bending at the poll. Nevertheless the effect of the mouthpiece itself is, exactly as on straight lines, a collecting one; the compacted inner side is held back to some extent and this allows the outer limbs to make a more ample gesture.

Using the curb with the intention of enforcing inflexion, correcting position and making the horse equilaterally pliant is an enterprise doomed to failure. Our forefathers knew this and used a cavesson for those purposes before the bridoon was invented.

However, the curb is a very powerful collecting instrument that in the past enabled riders to control their mount with one hand, leaving the other free for other uses. The reins were always held in one hand in those times when horses were bitted with only a curb mouthpiece.

When it became customary to adjoin a bridoon to the curb, partly to alleviate the severity of the latter, partly to put at the rider's disposal a suitable instrument for imposing turns and bending by means of the reins on horses who had not been sufficiently trained to obey the directions of seat and legs alone, all four reins would be held in one hand whenever the other hand had to remain free for other uses. At other times, the left hand, or bridle hand, held both curb reins and one bridoon rein; the other bridoon rein would normally be held in the right hand but, when necessary, could easily be transferred to the bridle hand. The switch was always carried in the right hand.

Such division of the reins has nowadays become unfashionable, and it seems to be the universal rule to divide the reins equally between both hands. There would be no disadvantage to this method of holding the reins if riders were always aware of the distinct functions and effects of the curb and bridoon. However, they seldom are and the consequence is that a large majority of horses resist the hand by stiffening the poll and the neck, going above or behind the bit, or manifesting their fear of the hand by the unsteadiness of their head carriage and by boring against the bit.

It is a fact that the reins are the first and indispensable means of teaching the young horse to go where his rider wants him to go; seat and legs can only be used to limited effect in those early stages of a horse's education. Subsequently, it must be mostly with his legs that the rider indicates bending and turning; but eventually a well trained horse should respond to the slightest seat effect and the legs can remain at the girth for the sole purpose of creating or preserving impulsion. In this final stage of a horse's education, when the slightest displacement of the rider's weight largely replaces the use of the legs for control of bend and direction, the role of the reins becomes paramount; however the horse must have become so pliant that the play of the fingers is sufficient to indicate direction and fulfil its role in collection.

Submission of this order can only be expected of a horse of Grand Prix class — a 'School Horse' in the old terminology; it cannot be required of what used to be known as a campaign horse. The idea that all horses can be controlled by subtle effects of seat, legs and hands is a dangerous delusion. Strong actions may be required in some cases, but then they can hardly be called 'aids'. A horse who has previously been ridden with a force measurable in kilos will have to undergo a long process of re-education before he can be controlled with delicate aids. This though seldom an impossible task, is always a lengthy one, rarely unattended by setbacks. Nevertheless, success in the enterprise makes all difficulties worthwhile.

Neither let us confuse normal rein aids with the powerful, energetic actions that may be required to overcome inattention, indifference, stubbornness or outright insubordination. The horse has to be absolutely convinced that the rider is master; he must accept his own subordinate place in the social order. A feeble or indulgent rider is a foolhardy rider. We must never forget that the horse is basically a herd animal and, in the herd, authority is based on respect for superior strength. If man willingly steps down from his rightful superior place in the social order understood by equines, he should not be surprised if his horse promptly climbs into the seat of power that he has irresponsibly vacated.

Many novice riders, and even some experienced ones, look upon the reins as their sole 'life-preserver' in critical moments. The reaction is a normal but primitive and dangerous reflex of self-defence and a blatant manifestation of feebleness. The best way to inhibit this dangerous reflex is to learn to sit correctly and discover the security and effectiveness of a correct seat.

In precarious situations the outcome depends entirely on the habit of obedience of the horse, an obedience which is developed, as already explained, by capitalizing on the laws of nature. Horses have minds of their own and when excited are capable of overriding the force of those laws; but although every occasion of excitement cannot be foreseen and avoided, a horse who has been properly trained into habits of obedience, and has learned to trust the rider's hand, will quickly forget the cause of his perturbation and regain his calm.

LEG AIDS

The legs are frequently said to be the seat of the soul of the rider. The truth is not so simple. *Legs which squeeze or knock, legs used too far behind the girth, or legs that grip to help the rider secure his position are certainly not aids.* The impulses of the legs are aids to efficient, regular movement only on condition that they do not oppose or disturb the natural rhythm of movement of the horse. The stimulating contacts of the legs with the horse's sides should be felt by the animal as impulses coming from the intrinsic regulator of movement in his own central nervous system. The position of the lower leg matters as much as the nature and rhythm of the impulses. Every unwarranted (frequently involuntary) change in the position of the lower leg signifies to the horse a change of intention on the part of the rider, a new command. If a rider has erratic legs, he should not be surprised to find his horse suddenly interrupting a particular exercise or starting on another that he had no intention himself of commanding.

It is sometimes necessary to use the leg in a punitive manner. However in this case, as in the case of all punitive actions, the intention must be purely to reinforce the aid: punishment must never become retaliation.

Legs which constantly knock are punishing legs,

and a horse treated in this manner will very soon become as dead to the leg as he can become hard mouthed as a result of constantly 'sawing' hands.

It is usual to distinguish between the forward driving and the guarding or restraining effect of the legs. However, the distinction applies to the purpose and manner of use and not to the position of the legs. In exactly the same place, a leg can be used alternatively as a forward driving influence or as a restraining influence.

Besides this distinction, another one should be made between the bending effect of the leg and its collecting effect, although in both cases the leg must also maintain its forward driving influence.

When a leg is used simultaneously to produce incurvation and maintain impulsion, its effect has to be reinforced by the reins because it is essential to prevent a localized bending of the longitudinal axis of the body. If the inside leg and inside rein alone were used to obtain the incurvation, the horse would bend at the withers and put his weight on his outside shoulder; hence the outside rein has to be used to limit the bending. On the other hand, in the absence of a restraining effect of the outside leg, the effect of the inside leg would cause the horse to pivot about this leg and turn his croup outward, but would not induce him to incurvate his body uniformly from head to tail.

Observing the movement from the ground, one can see whether the horse is correctly bent by watching the path of the limbs; the hind feet ought to step exactly in the traces of the forefeet.

It has already been pointed out that constantly pressing legs destroy the sensitivity of the horse's skin and thus cease to be aids. Similarly, the un-remitting pressure of the inside leg does not help the horse to understand what is required; it just annoys or alarms him. The bending effect of the inside leg is produced by intermittent very short, very brisk pressures at the rhythm of the gait. To give the inside leg the strength required, the hip joint on the same side must be well braced and the heel depressed (more weight on the inside stirrup); it is equally important to feel the right moment for the action and also the appropriate measure of firmness of the pressure.

Maintaining an unremitting pressure of the leg, besides annoying the horse, wastes the rider's energy, and it is important always to have enough energy in reserve for those moments when it is necessary to weaken the force of resistance of the horse. Riders who use totally unnecessary strength to maintain impulsion at times when no special demand has to be made on the horse will never have a reserve of force available for obtaining obedience when the horse resists the action of the leg. In transitions to canter, for example, the lower leg has to be properly positioned, ready for action; it need not, however, be used with particular emphasis except in certain movements such as counter-canter, or canter-renvers or -travers to produce the engagement of the inside hind.

It must also be imprinted upon the rider's mind that, however great the 'strength of the leg', it will always be completely ineffectual if other conditions prevail that invalidate its use, such as, for instance, an incorrect seat.

Most riders will have been taught that the most

effective spot for the forward driving influence of the leg is just behind the girth, and that the place for the restraining or sideways impelling leg is about a hand's breadth behind this spot. Still there are many riders who believe that the further back they act with their legs, the better they can 'drive the horse from behind'. In so doing, they reveal their ignorance of the locomotor system of the horse and they also defeat their object. If they do succeed in applying the pressure of their legs to the region of the false ribs, behind the true ribs, the pressure becomes not just less effectual, but the very reverse of impulsive. It makes the horse feel suffocated and less inclined to move forward, and the unpleasant sensation can cause him to run backwards and, in extreme cases, to rear.

The expression 'driving from behind' is somewhat misleading; it is quite impossible to push a horse forwards with the legs. What the pressures of the legs actually cause is a nervous impulse which produces a reflex contraction of certain muscles which extends to the musculature of the hindquarters. If the pressure occurs at the end of the period of retraction of a hind limb, at the moment when the foot is about to be lifted, it determines greater engagement of that hindleg during the subsequent period of protraction of the limb. Effectiveness does not therefore depend upon the strength of the rider but on his ability to feel the right moment and place at which to apply, with the requisite amount of energy, the pressure of the leg to trigger that reflex.

As regards the sideways driving leg, I repeat that it can be obeyed by the horse only on condition that it is not contradicted by the wrong weight effect.

If it is supported by correct seat and rein effects, very little strength is needed to determine the appropriate reaction on the part of the horse. In fact, a horse who has been properly trained to submit to the aids requires nothing more compelling by way of a sideways driving leg aid than a light 'stirrup aid' (pressure of the toe on the stirrup) to continue the lateral movement in which he had been engaged.

This aid must be accompanied by increased pressure of the seat bone on the same side. The effect on the horse is to cause the diagonal outside hind/inside fore pair of limbs to support for a very short moment a greater share of the load, thus allowing the opposite diagonal to advance more freely. At the very next step, the weight aid is reversed and the horse will continue to move forwards on two tracks without the rider having to use his outside leg actively. It is only in the stages of teaching the horse to understand the rider's intention that the outside leg may have to exert a certain amount of pressure somewhat behind the girth.

The leg aids for canter are also based on physical laws. The restraining outside leg (together with the outside rein) holds the outside shoulder of the horse for a moment, thus freeing the inside shoulder. The inside leg, just behind the girth, encourages the advance of the inside shoulder. It is in this manner that the horse is aided to start the canter. In theory, each spring of the canter has to be determined by the same aids; in practice however the leg aids need only be sufficiently energetic to be felt by the horse if the rider feels that the 'springs of the motor' are slackening; a good rider will act in good time to prevent a breaking of the canter.

In the flying change, it is during the period of suspension that the horse must change leads. The aids for the change must therefore coincide with this period. At the moment of suspension, outside leg and outside rein must restrain the new outside shoulder for a fraction of a second; the opposite shoulder is then free to advance. The horse is then incited to change lead and is urged to spring into the new canter by the new inside leg coming to its position at the girth. The difficulties experienced by many riders in teaching their horses to execute a flying change are frequently due to wrong timing of the aids. However when the change is difficult to one side only, this is because the horse has not yet been sufficiently straightened and is insensitive to the outside leg aid.

The legs can also have a collecting effect whenever it is necessary to warn the horse that he must gather himself in preparation for a different movement, for example walk pirouettes, rein-back, all transitions from the halt and of course the piaffe (and the levade which evolves from the piaffe).

It undoubtedly requires considerable skill to teach a horse to understand the collecting leg effect (which has of course to be supported by a particularly deep seat and a very quiet holding hand). In order to produce this effect the legs should act very discreetly in a vibrating manner somewhere in between their forward driving and their restraining positions; their pressures should not be absolutely simultaneous, but must alternate rapidly. The aid should be completely invisible to a spectator and must induce the horse to slightly take back his centre of gravity in relation to his base of support. The extent of the backward displacement of the centre of gravity must depend on the movement required. It should be minimal and almost imperceptible for a rein-back or a walk pirouette, at most producing a certain inner tension or concentration of force. Beyond a certain measure, it must perforce cause a compression of the hind joints which cannot be sustained for any length of time. Frequently the horse will relieve the discomfort of this compression of the hind joints by making a small spring forwards. On no account should he evade the discomfort by running backwards.

To conclude this discussion of the leg aids, it may be helpful to remind the reader of the rules governing the use of the legs.

1) The pressure of the legs should not normally be absolutely simultaneous. The time interval between the pressure of one leg and of the other is variable and depends on circumstances. However, simultaneous symmetrical action of both legs may occasionally be necessary to rouse attention or to punish.
2) The intensity of the leg impulses has to depend on the quickness of the horse's intelligence (no horse is actually thick-skinned). The aim should always be to use the minimal amount of energy necessary to produce the desired result.
3) The timing of the leg pressures must harmonize with the natural rhythm of movement of the horse. This can easily be sensed by the rider if his legs always remain easily in contact with the horse's ribcage in order to feel the expansion and contraction of the ribs that accompany the movements of the limbs.
4) The effect of the leg on the movement of a limb

73

during its phase of propulsion is nil. The horse can obey the leg only when a hindfoot is about to be picked up or is already off the ground.

5) The position of the lower legs is very important. Riders who hold their legs too far behind the girth produce horses who hold back on them.

6) The activity of the legs cannot compensate for a crooked seat or a faulty weight effect.

7) It may be necessary to emphasize that 'leg' means shank; the part of the leg between the knee and the ankle. The thighs have no function other than to help stabilize the rider's position by their friction with the saddle, and this function is best fulfilled by total relaxation of the muscles of the medial side of the thighs.

8) The inner surface of the knee on the saddle has to prevent gripping with the calves.

9) The power of the forward driving inside leg is obtained by depressing the heel and not by tightening the muscles at the back of the knee. With contracted leg muscles it is quite imposible either to 'bend' the horse or to feel the rhythm.

Wrong leg actions (with the exception of the disastrous grip with the calves) may have less dire consequences than wrong seat or rein effects, but they confuse the horse who will become more or less insensitive to their indications.

The spur is generally considered to be an aid but its wrong use provokes adverse results. It is not, in any case, a forward driving aid; used with adroitness, the spur is a collecting aid, a means of 'rounding the horse' or, in other words, of 'putting the horse in hand'. A horse can be said to be 'in hand' (on the bit) when he bridles correctly, and this is the criterion of proper use of the aids, spurs included. A horse is 'in hand' when he flexes the poll unresistingly and allows the rein effects to pass through the whole length of his body to all the joints of the hind limbs. For this purpose the rider can use the spur actively, with delicate prods, to improve lightness, or passively, letting the horse just feel the presence of the spur, reminding him to remain in suitable equilibrium. In both cases the spurs act by pressure and should not hit.

Although I have said that the spurs are not aids to impulsion, it is sometimes permissible to hit the horse with the spur, to punish him and mercilessly urge him onwards. Obviously such drastic action would be justified only in cases of gross idleness or outright resistance to the leg. However in principle it is absolutely wrong to use the spur systematically rather than the leg as an aid to impulsion.

For good riders spurs are steely reinforcement of leg aids to be held in reserve just in case the authority of the legs has to be strongly impressed upon the horse; alternatively they may use the spur tactfully to signal to the horse that he should collect himself in preparation for a particular exercise.

There are as many different kinds and shapes of spurs as ways of using them. The spur must be of a shape that allows it to make sufficient impression yet does not distress or wound the horse. The most effective spur is probably that which incorporates a small wheel rather than rowels; if rowels are felt to be necessary, their tips must be blunted.

There are riders who use their spurs to terrify the horse into abject submission (and frequently reinforce its effect by adjoining a tightly adjusted noseband to the curb). The spur can then hardly be described as an aid. Horses treated in this manner never lose their fear of this instrument of torture and never relax. It is usually very difficult if at all possible to get them to go genuinely on the bit. Such practices are totally opposed to the spirit of classical dressage, the aim of which is to obtain the horse's willing submission and to make him pliant by means of rational gymnastic exercises. The ambition to succeed in competition by hook or by crook leads to complete perversion of the art of dressage.

ARTIFICIAL AIDS

While on the subject of the aids it would be very remiss to ignore the artificial aids. Innumerable artificial aids have been devised throughout the history of horsemanship. Many were hailed overnight as being the perfect solution to all problems, and were discarded just as promptly. Some are still used at present without much thought being given as to whether they are appropriate. New ones will certainly come and go but one thing only is certain, which is that *there is no artificial aid that can lastingly replace the skilful use of the direct aids of reins, weight and legs of the rider.*

One or another of the artificial aids may be usefully resorted to for a while to reinforce the effect of the direct aids provided that the rider does not come to rely on it entirely and uses it with prudence and understanding. On the other hand, a rider who relies more on these 'dead' instruments than on his own 'live' forces will never succeed in establishing a satisfactory rapport with his horse.

Even at the risk of being considered eccentric, I

maintain that one should never employ artificial aids (or special bits) at the beginning of training. Some old textbooks may well devote whole chapters to the use of various artificial aids, but the mere fact that so many are described proves that none was entirely serviceable.

Work in hand, touching certain parts of the horse's body with a switch, is a method sometimes advocated in the advanced education of the horse to get him to understand clearly what he is required to do. One should be warned that this method is fraught with dangers; the inexpert trainer can do far more harm in this manner than he can do with direct aids when he is mounted.

One of the objects of work in hand may be to gain time by familiarizing the horse with a particularly difficult movement – piaffe for example – before trying to teach this from the mounted position. Even if it can be assumed that the horse is mentally and physically capable of executing the movement, exceptionally good powers of observation are required; one has to find the right spot to touch and, more important still, the right moment at which to apply the touch. Moreover, the horse still has to learn to perform the movement in obedience to the direct aids and, if he had first been drilled in hand, the assistance of the trainer on the ground may be required for a long time before the animal can learn to associate the direct aids of the rider with the indirect aids of the trainer.

At other times work in hand is used to intensify the gymnastic flexing of the hind joints. With a horse who is sufficiently advanced in his gymnastic training, this procedure has certain advantages.

Simultaneous flexion of all the joints of the loaded hind limb is strenuous, and it is understandable that a horse should at times feel less than enthusiastic about doing gymnastics of this kind even when it is not painful. In natural movement, horses avoid this uneconomical effort except when they play or are driven by superabundant energy, such as the sexual instinct or the need to defeat a rival. It is therefore perfectly understandable that one should frequently have to use more stringent aids than those of the legs to persuade the horse to work in this unusual manner, but one ought to understand that lack of enthusiasm for energetic gymnastics is not the same thing as resistance. Stubborn resistance is usually the consequence of human lack of understanding of the nature of the animal.

Work in hand can be a useful method in the advanced education of the horse, but it must be prepared and completed by mounted work with correct use of the direct aids of seat and legs. (If the purpose of work in hand is to awaken the horse's ardour, it is of course essential to accustom him prudently to the sight and feel of the switch; a startled horse would react to the touches of the switch in a very disconcerting manner for his rider.) Excessive reliance on work in hand has often resulted in a horse's complete contempt for the direct aids and considerable humiliation for the rider when the horse, realizing that assistance from the ground is no longer available to the person on his back, digs in his toes and remains resolutely 'at the post', completely unmoved by the frantic efforts of the rider.

In order to avoid finding oneself exposed to such humiliation, it is essential to learn how to galvanize

Ganhe Capriole gerade vor sich.
La Capriole entière sur la ligne.
N.º 43.

J. E. R.

the horse from a seated position when his spirit flags. Horses are perfectly capable of feeling when the rider means business and when he is prepared to tolerate a certain degree of laxity, provided that they are taught often enough to respond promptly to more pressing leg aids.

The most suitable instrument for activating the hindquarters is a switch just long enough to allow the rider to touch one or another part of the hind-quarters with precision and from a sufficiently safe distance. The switch should be fairly rigid, except towards the tip. Too whippy a switch would make it difficult to touch the right spot at the right moment. If the touches are applied at the wrong moment and on the wrong spot they can easily provoke excitement and defeat their object. Although it may sometimes be necessary to deliberately excite the horse, this should be a result of conscious choice, and not of human error.

Trainers experienced at work in hand have found out that the most suitable spot to touch varies between individual horses and that the sensitivity of individuals is also variable. There are horses, and not necessarily spoilt ones, who are remarkably impassive and will respond only to energetic use of the switch. Others are so sensitive that the slightest hint of a touch, or just the sight of the switch can produce intense reaction.

The method can be attended by such untoward results that it is better to leave it to real experts unless one has a particularly well-developed psychological sense allied with considerable adroitness. I am not against work in hand on principle, but I want to stress that satisfactory results can be expected only if the trainer has outstanding empathy, sound knowledge and great experience. Inexpert work in hand easily produces a spoilt horse.

Work in the pillars is a special form of work in hand, but I need only discuss it briefly since there are few private training establishments that are equipped with pillars; even the Spanish Riding School of Vienna has discarded them.

In the past, work in the pillars was used as a very effective means of developing the strength of the hindquarters and teaching the piaffe from the outset, but the horses would have had to possess an appropriate conformation to produce a correct piaffe. The type of riding horse preferred nowadays has a more oblong frame than the horses used in the classical period and has the centre of gravity rather more forward; his hind limbs are not designed to support a major proportion of the body weight and to flex the joints in the manner described as 'setting the horse on the haunches', even though this is still a requirement for a correct piaffe as laid down by the F.E.I. Modern dressage horses are required to do movements which were not demanded of the old-fashioned type and, if one wishes to develop to the full their capacity for spectacular extended movements, one may on the other hand have to be content with an engagement of hocks that does not entirely meet the requirements laid down by the F.E.I. There are exceptions of course, but on the whole a perfectly classical piaffe is too difficult for them.

Conformation and the consequent ability of the joints of the hind limbs to flex deeply determined the horse's psychological adaptation to work in the pillars. Since the pillars to which he was attached prevented forward movement, the touches of the switch would compel the horse to engage his hind limbs under his centre of gravity and flex simultaneously all the joints. Such are the conditions of a perfect piaffe; the lowering of the haunches resulting in a corresponding lightening of the forehand, which, in turn, permitted a lifting of the forearms to the horizontal. It is this elevation of the forearms that imparts grace to the movement and puts the horse in the class known as the High School.

Work in the pillars allowed the trainer to supervise the reactions of the horse and prevent any evasive action of the hindquarters, such as lifting the croup or lateral deviations. The carriage of the whole body could be improved without straining the ligaments of the hind joints.

It is undeniable that a correct piaffe gives a horse an impressive appearance and is the sign of a highly polished education. Nevertheless, it was always recognized that work in the pillars could have some serious drawbacks which, in addition to the fact that pillars are no longer available except in very few private establishments, are the reasons for its disuse.

To conclude this short discussion on the subject of artificial aids, I have to say that correctly conducted work in hand can be useful but it can never be a panacea and can never replace mounted work. One should not spend more time on it than may be necessary to help the horse to understand the rider's intention. Once this object has been achieved, it is from the saddle with the direct aids of seat, legs and hands that the rider must continue the education of his horse.

Education of the Horse

At the start of this chapter it is necessary to point out that technical competence is not enough to guarantee successful education of a young horse or successful further education of a schooled horse. It must also be emphatically stressed that every stage of the horse's education has to be entirely confirmed before embarking on the next one. Uncorrected faults and irregularities soon set limits on further progress; every stage has to be built on a perfectly sound foundation. It is only if the rider has educated himself to recognize at each stage the relevant criteria of correct performance that he will know whether the time is ripe to introduce new difficulties. Every step is a milestone on the way to the final goal; skipping a step is simply a waste of time (and money) and definitely compromises one's chances of achieving one's aim.

It has often been believed that schooling had to be adapted to the contemplated ultimate utilization of the horse. In reality, the principles are the same for all horses; the important thing is the systematic progression from one stage to the next and observance of the criteria that apply to each of them.

One thing holds good for all degrees of education; the willing consent of the horse has first to be obtained and then carefully preserved. Coercion at first agitates a horse, subsequently, on the contrary, it causes lethargy or even stubborn resistance. It never produces high achievement and for rider and spectator it spoils the enjoyment of the sport.

If the rider or trainer has a modicum of psychological sense and never overtaxes the horse's physical and mental aptitudes he should not find it particularly difficult to gain the animal's trust and cooperation.

84

Unfailing patience is the best guarantee of success. It is understandable that one should lose one's cool at times particularly if one is young or naturally excitable, but every temporary loss of self-control entails a greater or smaller set-back in the progress of the horse's education. No rider will be completely spared occasional moments of exasperation, so it is important to acknowledge this and train oneself to try to remain self-possessed in all circumstances; causes of annoyance will then become less frequent.

An old and wise rule states that a horse should never be sent back to the stable with the memory of an upsetting conclusion to the lesson fresh in his mind. However, there are occasions when the rule has to be bent to state that 'It is always better to put up with an unsatisfactory outcome of a training session than to allow one's temper or impatience to turn the agitation of the horse into outright rebellion; the lesson can be resumed in the next training period when one has regained one's composure and had time to think of a new and better way of solving a frustrating problem'.

Since the aptitudes of individual trainers and individual horses are variable, it should be evident that the course and length of training will vary in each case. Nevertheless, the same basic principles apply to them all.

Riders and horses may differ, nevertheless, regardless of the exceptionally promising aptitudes of a horse, one should not resort to methods that violate the nature of the animal. Certain forceful procedures may impress onlookers but ultimately they do not produce better results than persevering practice of progressively difficult exercises.

A sensible attitude to dressage education will ensure that a trainer with limited experience will avoid using certain methods that depend for their success upon the skill of an expert. It is in any case important to have a good measure of modesty; creativity enters into the art of dressage, but one must be prepared to accept stern criticism of one's own ideas or practices if it becomes apparent that they can be harmful to the welfare of horse or rider.

The character and disposition of a horse of any age are tremendously influenced by the attitude of his trainer and rider who is responsible for the psychological education of the animal throughout the various stages of training. As regards physical education, this has to start with the horse's earliest endeavours to maintain his balance under the disturbing influence of the rider's weight.

It is impossible to be precise about the age at which a horse is ready to be ridden because growth and strength vary considerably between the different breeds; in general however three or four years old is the lowest limit for the start of work education. Riding a horse under this age amounts to 'child labour' and, with few exceptions, leads to premature unfitness for work. The psychological damage is also serious but this is seldom mentioned.

Three or four (although three is often too early), is the best age to start introducing the saddle horse to education. Yet, although the animal may outwardly appear fully grown, one must remember that he is not yet physically mature. The joints of the vertebral column and limbs are not completely formed nor are they adequately protected by the muscles and ligaments which control their movements. Overwork at an early age is the root cause of many an unsoundness which may not manifest itself until some years later. *All work with a young horse — or with a horse that has not yet been ridden — must be enlightened by consideration of his psychological and physical constitution.* This signifies that, at the beginning, one must be prepared to accept what he willingly offers, and not surprise him with bewildering demands.

Prudence should not, however, deter one from starting the education of the horse while he is young. It is absolutely essential to imprint on the animal mind from the very start consciousness of the superior status and indisputable authority of the rider. Every moment of weakness on the part of the rider naturally muddles the equine brain and unnecessarily complicates relations between man and horse.

As soon as the horse has learnt to cope with the weight of the rider (and most horses learn this quickly) and with due consideration for his physical and mental preparedness, one can proceed to introduce carefully and progressively rather more difficult schooling movements.

Every new demand of the rider will naturally be met by some measure of opposition from the horse. An absolutely indisputable rule is that *it is always the rider's will that must prevail. This does not at all invalidate the previously stated necessity of consideration for the horse's mental and physical powers.*

The two most important impulses of the horse are firstly a desire to go forward and secondly an instinctive objection to domination by another creature. The desire to go forwards is not normally a problem if the horse is strong enough to carry the rider and is given time to recover his natural equilibrium under the additional weight of the latter. However, the human requirements of manoeuvrability automatically impose upon the animal a rather unnatural use and development of the muscular power of the hindquarters. The necessary gymnastic training – even if it is managed prudently by the rider – initially entails for the horse an effort that he would avoid making in natural conditions, since it would be an uneconomical utilization of his propulsive forces. It is therefore understandable that the horse should, at times, manifest at least a degree of agitation if not outright resistance when required to make what represents in his mind an unnecessarily strenuous effort. If, at this stage, *the rider is* unreasonably *demanding, the horse soon realizes that obedience entails worrying discomfort and develops the habit of arguing.* However, constant abdication by the rider merely postpones the altercation which will be all the more vehement the longer it is deferred. It is therefore essential for the rider or trainer to oppose the horse's wilfulness with calm and resolution until he gives up resistance and understands that he is duty bound to execute the movement required.

There are various ways of teaching a horse to accept the presence of a rider on his back and any that does not alarm the horse unduly (or better still does not alarm him at all) is acceptable. Some horses are inordinately sensitive, and it may be necessary in such cases to proceed with special forethought and for the rider himself to do the first mounting rather than let someone else get astride. Rough and ready 'breaking-in' by methods intended to break the horse's spirit completely are reprehensible. In any case rough breaking-in does not always achieve its purpose and frequently provokes more or less pronounced reactions of self-defence which will persist throughout the whole of the horse's education.

STARTING WORK

Should the horse be worked on the lunge before the first mounting lessons? Ought the first mounted lessons be conducted on the lunge or on a long rein attached to a leading horse? There is no rule. The answer is usually dictated by training facilities and custom. Any one of the usual procedures is valid so long as it respects the animal's psychological make-up.

However, there is no doubt that lungeing the horse prior to his first mounted lesson has advantages, provided that the lungeing lessons are carefully started and carried out. Correct lungeing accustoms the horse to the habit of work and develops trust in the rider. With the help of side reins and the whip one can get the horse to reach for the bit and develop impulsion with little risk of his getting away.

Nevertheless, work on the lunge, whether in the initial period of training or at any later time, must always be conducted with intelligent precautions. I cannot warn too strongly against the adverse consequences of allowing a young horse to run on a circle, dragging the trainer at the other end of the lunge line. A training surcingle or saddle, and properly adjusted side reins and cavesson are essential equipment.

When the horse has learnt to accept without fuss the presence of a rider on his back, and outside control by the lunge or other means can safely be dispensed with, at first the only aids at the disposal of the rider will be the reins. At this time, the horse should be ridden as much as possible on straight lines because seat and leg effects at this stage can easily alarm him. One should not of course expect wonders from the rein aids. It is with the inside 'opening' rein that changes of direction are indicated and, at the beginning, there are no counter measures available to the rider if the horse resists the turning indication of the inside rein by putting his weight onto his outside shoulder.

It is unhesitating forward movement and acceptance of contact that will show that the horse has learnt to move confidently with a rider in the saddle. However, at this stage, it would be foolish to expect him to move in horizontal equilibrium. Instead, the horse must be allowed to carry a somewhat greater proportion of weight on the forehand and to use his hind legs entirely for their natural propulsive function.

When calm forward movement and confident contact have been achieved, the time has come to start influencing the mechanism of motion by careful use of combined seat, leg and rein effects. Part of every lesson should be devoted to teaching the horse to move with shorter steps. Short active steps strengthen the hind limbs, whereas trying to lengthen the strides at this stage would put the horse even more on the forehand.

No more difficult form of gymnastic training of the hind limbs should be considered for the next six months. However, during this time the horse can be taught to lengthen and lower his neck and apply some tension to the reins, and to obey the restraining outside leg and the direct inside rein on large circles and in changes of direction.

Whenever the horse puts up resistance the rider must, before firmly repressing it, ascertain its cause. He may have overestimated the horse's physical or mental aptitudes, in which case he will have to moderate his demands. On the other hand it may be that the horse has discovered the superiority of his strength and the ways in which he can disobey the rider's commands; in which case he must immediately be brought back to order and made to feel that his obedience must be unconditional.

The rider's countermeasures must of course be commensurate with the degree of disobedience of the horse; one does not use heavy artillery to shoot at sparrows. *However, a horse should never be allowed to find out that he can get away with any manifestation of wilfulness. Indulgence and compromise are methods that are sometimes advocated in the education of children (with doubtful results); in our relations with equines they always have disastrous consequences. Undoing the damage caused by a rider's weakness and lasting forbearance is always a difficult and lengthy task.*

The first psychological aid of the rider is recognition of the fact that it is in the nature of horses to bow to the superiority of strength. Already in the first year of life, foals herded at pasture constantly engage in apparently playful activities which are in reality trials of strength and resolution. We can certainly not allow the much stronger three- or four-year-old youngster to imagine that he will be allowed to play the same sort of game with his human attendant, trainer or rider.

From the very outset of training, the rider (without forgetting his own obligations) has to convince the horse of his reasonable but unquestionable authority. If he tolerates any form of disrespect on the part of the animal, it will not be long before the roles of master and servant are reversed. Having discovered the weakness of the supposed boss, the horse will almost certainly arrogate the superior position on all occasions of conflicting intentions.

However, it is most unlikely that any rider is prepared to acknowledge that it is his permissiveness which has sown the seeds of disobedience in his horse's mind to the extent of making the animal totally unsuitable for any of the various disciplines, and the importance of obedience in the early stages of training is unfortunately not sufficiently realized.

ELEMENTARY EDUCATION

After the first period of getting the horse used to the task of carrying a rider, the elementary education of the animal includes a number of requirements that must be satisfied before the horse can be considered sufficiently obedient to allow one to go on to training at medium or 'campaign' level.

The first requirement is pliancy; the horse has to be taught to incurvate his body according to the curving of the track. All horses are stiffer on one side than the other, a fact that very soon becomes evident to a sensitive rider. The first task therefore is to equalize lateral flexibility as much as possible. In the majority of cases, this is by no means an easy task, but it nevertheless cannot be postponed; when a horse has developed the habit of moving more or less crookedly he becomes extremely difficult to straighten and the muscles of the weaker and less elastic side become increasingly stiff.

Equal compliance to the right and left aids of legs and reins is an absolute condition for advanced dressage training.

It is a well known fact that all movements with

left dorsal incurvation are easier to obtain than those with right incurvation. In fact the soft or 'hollow' side is the more difficult one to work on. There are many recipes for the correction of one-sided stiffness; the apparent contradictions just prove that the training of all horses cannot conform to a stereotyped pattern. Within the limits of the inviolate basic principles, the intelligent and creative horseman will adopt the method best suited to the individual case, but will never resort to cruel and inept means of coercion for he will know that they cannot achieve his purpose.

In addition to teaching a horse to incurvate himself on circles it is also essential to teach him to move straight on straight lines. In many cases the purpose of incurvation is to put the horse in such a position that he has to accept the collecting aids of the rider. Straightness on the other hand is an essential condition of correct gaits, but a horse will not move perfectly straight until he obeys right and left diagonal hand and leg aids equally without fuss. Incurvation implies submission to rein and leg aids (supported of course by the seat effect); hence until correct incurvation can be obtained in work on circles, it is not possible to get the horse to move straight on straight lines.

Straight forward movement was regarded by the masters of the past as an absolutely essential condition of submission. It is just as essential to understand *how* one teaches a horse to move straight. Attempting to correct the natural bend of all horses by the use of strongly coercive auxiliary reins is curing one evil by resorting to a worse one since it induces a hypertension that spoils impulsion and regularity even more than does the natural crookedness.

Additionally, direct (vertical) flexion of the poll

must be obtained at this stage of the horse's education. This is an important element of submission, for it is not possible to influence the flexion of the hind joints if the rein effects stop at the withers as the result of a wrong position of head and neck. *Far too many riders continue to confuse collection and submission of the poll and neglect to cultivate the suppleness of the poll until they start working on the collected gaits.*

Direct flexion at the poll may be difficult for some horses either because of unfavourable conformation of the two first cervical vertebrae or because of the shape of the mandible and resulting compression of the parotid glands. Such disadvantages have to be neutralized as soon as possible.

If a horse finds out that he can spare himself inconvenient effort behind by refusing to yield at the poll, his obedience will always depend upon his mood. He will always be able to evade the generally collecting effect of the aids and any corrective measures attempted by the rider will be fruitless.

However most resistances to flexion of the poll stem from the stiffness or weakness of the hindquarters rather than from the conformation of the mandible or the upper cervical vertebrae and it is impossible to overcome resistance if its actual source is wrongly identified. Stiffening of the poll rooted in stiffness of the hind joints cannot be corrected by the hand.

Similarly, pliancy of the poll has to go hand-in-hand with a corresponding activity of the hindquarters. Hence one should not demand utmost flexion of the poll before the muscles of the hindquarters have acquired sufficient strength and elasticity. Trying to impose an ideal head position with the reins alone, without consideration of the engagement of the hind limbs, usually results in dangerously exaggerated bridling or overbending, that is to say a break in the curve of the neck behind the two first vertebrae that form the poll. Both faults shorten the frame in a useless manner and prevent effective control of the hindquarters.

Flexion of the poll and compacting of the frame has to be the *result* of impulsion; it has to come from behind and not the other way round by enforcing with a vertical position of the nose the aid of the reins.

It is well known that, with adroit manipulation of reins, a rider who is just a good artisan can show a well-schooled horse to advantage, but one needs to be a genuine artist to introduce a horse to new difficulties without spoiling his disposition, and technical competence alone does not guarantee that a rider will be capable of educating every young horse with the same likelihood of success.

For horses, even more than for humans, the final result of schooling depends on a good start. One of the strongest characteristics of horses is their remarkable impressionability, especially in the early stages of their education when their mind has to interpret the meaning of completely novel and strange impressions. The rider must be aware of the fact that too many strange sensations suddenly crowding the horse's mind can be very detrimental to the smooth course of training.

To begin with, most young horses will react positively to the startling effect of the rider's aids and will comply with his demands if it is within their capacity to do so. However, each horse soon seeks various ways of lessening the effort required to conform with the rider's wishes.

If the rider is deceived by the almost humanly sly means of defence employed by the horse to avoid honest work, faults will insidiously develop, and will be all the more difficult to correct the longer they are overlooked. But if the rider realizes that the principal object of every schooling session during this period of education must be the gymnastic development of the hindquarters, he will not be likely to allow faults to become established.

The consequent unloading of the forehand does not only prolong the soundness of the forelimbs, it also promotes better related activity of the back muscles and equilibrium. As cadence develops, rider and horse will increasingly present the picture of easiness, grace and harmony which should be the mark of dressage training.

Regarding the aids, the role of the seat together with the legs is to foster the energetic picking up of the hind feet, promoting the elasticity of ligaments and the strength of muscles which will enable the horse to flex painlessly all the joints of the increasingly loaded hind limbs.

The hands, for their part, should be as steady and passive as possible, they must however allow the horse to put an elastic tension on the reins; at this stage he needs this assistance to preserve his equilibrium. In the corners of the manege and on the circle they must also help the horse to incurvate his body correctly. At a much later stage, when the hind limbs have acquired the necessary strength to be well engaged, it is with his hands that the rider assists the horse in converting some of what was initially the purely propulsive role of the hind limbs into a more supportive one, inducing him also to use his back muscles increasingly to that end.

It is wrong to induce flexion of the poll by constant interference with the hands; this always results in an unsteady neck carriage. If the rider can learn instead to feel the correct activity of the hind limbs, he will easily develop the feel of a suitable tension of the reins. His hands will also then develop the feel of the movement and acquire the steadiness that is much more helpful to the horse than their ceaseless busyness.

Correct positioning and incurvation on turns and circles entail increased activity of the inside hindleg, and unless he is suitably positioned and incurved, the horse cannot preserve his equilibrium during such movements. However it ought to be clearly understood that neither position nor incurvation can be imposed by the hands, both have to be the result of the influence of the seat and of the impulsive effect of the legs.

The young horse should be ridden to start with in a correct light seat. The light seat accustoms the horse more easily to the presence of a rider on his back; the full or heavy seat might frighten the horse because it is not always possible at this stage to avoid an unbalancing uneven loading of the three points of the base of support.

Very soon however, one should introduce the horse to the feel of the full seat, at least for short periods of time; one of the reasons being that the full seat is essential for maintenance of impulsion at the canter. Of course, the canter is not a suitable gait for the initial stages of schooling; the horse's hind limbs are not yet strong enough and the firm leg pressures needed to sustain the gait can alarm the horse. However, once the horse accepts the aid of the legs without fuss and remains in balance when the rider sits to the trot, the canter can be introduced for short periods of time.

A word now about the walk. Much importance is rightly attached to the purity and scope of this gait, and an experienced buyer will always observe the walk of a horse with great attention. However, he may not again devote the same attention to the gait during training until the horse is about to be presented in a dressage test, at which juncture he will usually have to admit that the walk has lost much of the quality that had struck him at the time of purchase.

However, the trainer or rider can gain assurance that he is proceeding on the right lines if the horse immediately returns to a correct, calm medium walk in perfect four-time after a session of demanding work. A correct walk is not conceivable if a horse has been submitted to harsh methods of constraint in his schooling.

The walk also helps to indicate whether a horse is using his back muscles as he should, and it reveals clearly the rider's own quality. The rider's seat cannot be correct if he has to use strong leg aids or the whip to urge the horse on or to regulate the gait.

Therefore, at no stage during the whole education of the horse should one neglect to observe the horse at the walk. The medium walk of the novice horse must be as correct as the walk of the Grand Prix horse. If the walk of the trained horse is not as good as it was before training, it is without doubt a rider who has spoilt it.

Riders cannot all be cast in the same mould; neither does a stereotyped pattern of training exist, but a rider gifted with particularly good feel will have less difficulty than most in getting the horse to understand his wishes, and will easily appreciate how much he can demand safely. Nevertheless he will have to beware of pressing on too quickly with the training of a keen horse whose joints may not yet be as strong as his enthusiasm. There is an old saying that lazy horses seldom become spavined. One should rejoice in the natural impulsion of a horse but it may often be necessary to moderate his desire to go forward.

There is no room here to enumerate all the criteria of correctness of work at this stage of training but a horse who has not received a thorough grounding in the basic elements of dressage education cannot be said to be truly rideable. The most favourable natural aptitudes of his mount do not absolve a rider from the necessity of proceeding systematically. Time spent on a good elementary education is never wasted, since it will greatly speed up progress in the next phase.

Loose schooling or riding over obstacles are not satisfactory substitutes for regular practise of the classical gymnastic exercises which so well develop the horse's body and have, for centuries, formed the basis of dressage training.

Regardless of a horse's talent, extraordinary performance cannot be expected of him unless he can call upon reserves of strength when faced with a particularly strenuous task. These reserves must be built up. If the horse does not possess them, urging him on to the very limit of his strength abuses his goodwill and compromises his soundness.

Formerly, horsemen were made very conscious of the capacity for work of their horses and were careful to foster and preserve it. Nowadays, unfortunately, not all riders are educated in horsemanship and it seems that more than a few have little sense of responsibility for the soundness of their partner in the sport. It is not right to demean the animal to the status of a mechanical instrument that has regularly to be tested to the limit of its capacity.

A rider who has ever had the good fortune of being offered a ride on a horse who has been soundly educated to a high degree of proficiency will most certainly be fired with the ambition to train his own horse (or one that has been entrusted to him for training) to the same level. The higher one aims, the greater the demands one must make on oneself. For the horseman at heart, the obligation is not irksome; there will be many moments of great joy which will be sufficient reward for the exacting self-discipline. One would have to be very insensitive not to feel considerable satisfaction every time a horse shows that he understands his rider's wishes and tries to oblige him.

If he aims for the top, the rider must, of course, be as accomplished as he expects his horse to be. Even for the layman the sight of ugly, inept riding of a superlative horse seriously detracts from enjoyment of the sport.

The art of horsemanship is not the preserve of the sport of dressage. Performance in the show-jumping ring can be marked by as much quality as in the dressage arena. What the genuine horse-loving spectator appreciates is a demonstration of complete harmony between horse and rider. I have never seen an equestrian statue representing the horse as an anxious and oppressed beast. The sculpture would be unacceptable to the public. The living picture of man and horse ought to be aesthetically pleasing also. It's a shame to realize how few riders nowadays share this view.

A training programme has, in any case, to be systematic; all education must be progressive and continuous, not only in duration but also in the sequence of exercises and difficulties. The aim is of course the development of the horse's potential, but it is the responsibility of the teacher to know his subject and to assess progress correctly. He must take into consideration the physical maturity of the animal, his conformation, temperament and degree of docility. The more accurate his estimation of those influences, the better will he succeed in smoothing the course of progress.

Muscular strength, for example, varies considerably from horse to horse despite similar appearances. Young and rather weak horses have to be treated with especial care; their periods of work must be short and their schooling undemanding. Robust young horses on the contrary can soon put up with fairly exacting work and they may frequently have to be made to feel the power of the aids. Mature horses who have not received any education should generally be treated as youngsters; just as much time will be required to strengthen their muscles, tendons and joints. The training of horses with a weakness of conformation requires a lot of patience and modest expectations. Capitalizing on their strong points helps to calm them down after they have become agitated by work intended to strengthen their weaknesses.

Temperament must also be taken into account. Impetuous horses should be relaxed by long periods of trotting on as long a rein as practical before they can be asked to work more or less collectedly. In their case the appropriate weapons are quietness and perseverance. Forcible bridling aggravates their impetuosity and the reins are of no avail when their temper has been roused. In such cases, it is important to discover the root cause of their resentment of control; it could be a rather unfavourable conformation of the top cervical vertebrae, tight spacing of the rami of the mandible and consequent painful compression of the parotid glands or, more commonly, just a weak back. If it is the leg aid they resent, quiet, free forward movement is again the most appropriate remedy.

On the contrary, lazy, phlegmatic horses must be stirred up by forceful means: legs, spurs or whip. They must be compelled to maintain an active, springy working trot before any more advanced movement is introduced.

Disposition also has a strong influence on the course of education. Good tempered horses rarely object to suppling exercises, while timid, apprehensive horses have to be reassured. Forceful aids increase their feeling of insecurity and in extreme cases can drive them crazy; they need a very quiet rider.

Calmness, coolness and perseverance, a particularly firm seat and very steady hands are needed with lively and excitable horses. They must be given long daily periods of quiet exercise and should not be granted a weekly day of rest.

However, the most resistant horses are the indolent ones. They retaliate against the use of legs, spurs or whip by lashing out with one or both hind legs. They need a very resolute, indomitable rider, determined to teach them respect for the aids. Of course

Halb lustig rechts gerade aus.
A demi allegre sur la ligne.
Nᵒ 35.

J. E. R.

laziness and exhaustion must not be confused; the first has to be met with forceful aids, the second with leniency.

Obviously the aids must always be consistent. Urging a horse on whilst simultaneously holding him back on too strong a rein contact, punishing at the same time with the spurs and a good sock in the mouth, will turn a merely lazy horse into a sulky one who holds his tail firmly clamped down between his buttocks and refuses to come up to the bit. Such contradictory aids are very frightening when they add to the pain caused by a stiff poll or a narrow mandible and they can only increase the horse's reluctance to go forward.

Fear of the legs can also be a cause of resistance. In the early stages of training, it may be necessary to displace the restraining outside leg backward a little (without lifting the knee or increasing pressure). If the horse objects, it is unwise to remove the leg contact immediately. When a horse overreacts to the outside leg, the best policy is to maintain its contact unchanged.

Obedience to the legs is the most important element of the horse's education. However, submission to the legs has to be built up progressively with reference to the horse's strength and intelligence; it cannot be obtained if too much is demanded at any stage of schooling, or if the reactions of the horse are misjudged, or, again, if necessary punishment is not commensurate with the degree of disobedience.

A horse can be considered to be obedient when he has been rationally trained to understand the meaning of the aids and has learnt to conform immediately and willingly to their indications, and when he is disposed, if necessary, to use every ounce of his reserves of energy to satisfy the rider's requirements.

The basic education is the same for all horses, but they do not all have to be trained to a very advanced degree of submission. However, those who show good aptitude for the special discipline of dressage will have to be put through further stages in their education. Moreover, the rider who wants to teach his horse lateral work, to perform repeated flying changes at canter and the other difficult movements required at Grand Prix level will also have to complete his own knowledge and improve his skill. The same applies to the show-jumping enthusiast. Ability to go with the horse over obstacles is not sufficient to ensure successful performance in major competitions. Exceptional skill and feeling are needed when it comes to placing a horse, to driving him forward between obstacles, to mobilizing all his forces in order to negotiate successfully the daunting combinations that will cross his path. If this were not the case, considering the potential number of really good horses, there would be far more participants in major show-jumping events.

Before starting his specialized education, a horse with favourable conformation and temperament for either advanced dressage or show-jumping or the three-day event will have to complete first a medium stage of schooling that will make him into what used to be called a 'campaign horse'. The expression indicated that the animal was a versatile, entirely dependable mount with enough quality to merit spending more time on schooling towards the special discipline for which he seemed best suited.

The aim of the previous stage was to develop prudently the general locomotor system of the animal. Now the exercises included in the programme of schooling are all designed to foster perfect self-carriage and pliancy and especially to develop the springiness and weight supporting capacity of the hind limbs; unless the muscles protecting the joints of the hind limbs are thoroughly trained, future athletic performance could seriously compromise the soundness of those joints.

Movements on two tracks are especially suited for the purpose and originally they were regarded just as a means towards the end; where they are required in modern dressage tests it is mainly because of their spectator appeal. It is, however, very important that the rider should understand the initial object of shoulder-in, travers, renvers and half-pass rather than considering them merely as sophisticated movements that have to be learnt because of their inclusion in various tests. Their usefulness is explained in all the serious books that have been written on the subject of dressage, and it is always with their true purpose in mind that we should proceed when teaching them to the horse.

Their correct execution involves a muscular effort much in excess of the one required for normal equine locomotion, and it is understandable that the horse should at first try various ways of outwitting the rider. The correctness of the latter's position and aids will therefore have to be frequently verified.

If the rider insisted from the outset on absolutely classical two-track movement, or persisted in his demands for unreasonably long periods of time, the horse would either find a deceptive way of shirking honest work or would openly put up resistance. Furthermore, his resentment of the effort would never diminish. It is, on the whole, better to out-smart the horse than to try to force execution of the movements by means of strong aids.

One should never forget that the lateral movements were designed to help strengthen the hind legs with a view to their role in collection. A big step forward will have been achieved when the horse starts showing real enjoyment of two-track work and is no longer conscious of the effort required. By contrast an unsympathetic, impatient rider, who has resorted to forceful aids during training, will be totally at the mercy of the horse's mood when he has to show these movements in a dressage test and he knows that his own position and aids are under scrutiny.

I should perhaps repeat my warning of the dis-advantages of indirect aids (such as touches of a switch by an assistant on the ground) principally because they are not available at crucial moments. They can be helpful only on condition that the rider learns to master as soon as possible the art of influencing the movement by the direct aids of seat, legs and hands.

Unity of mind of horse and rider is not an empty phrase. It is a highly possible and worthwhile aim which can be achieved if a rider understands that the aids are influences rather than irresistible mechanical effects, uses them adroitly at the right moment and does not make unreasonable demands of the animal's mental and physical powers.

The flying change must also be taught during this

stage of schooling. Although horses will change legs fluently when they gallop at pasture, they usually find changes difficult when they have to carry a rider at the canter. Overcoming the difficulty can be the most trying lesson of the training programme.

This goes to show — since the movement is such a natural one for the horse — that it is not so easy for the rider to learn to move in perfect unison with the horse at the rhythm of canter. At the stage of teaching the horse to understand the requirement, it needs only a minute delay in giving the aids or the smallest discord of aids to make the change difficult or impossible for the horse. Later, when he has learnt to understand the message, the slightest indication will be sufficient to get him to execute the movement, and he may even perform a correct change despite inadequate aids.

Learning to communicate clearly with the horse, without garbling the message by using discrepant aids, is a difficult lesson for riders who have slow reflexes. After years of practise, they may acquire a certain mechanical ability but it can only partly replace natural talent. *Exaggerated seat, leg or rein influences are extremely detrimental to the fluency of the change. They compromise the horse's equilibrium and cannot therefore be called aids.*

In the case of a horse with the right aptitudes for advanced dressage, it is important to introduce — with prudence — the difficulties of this exacting discipline while he is still learning to become just a good 'campaign horse'. The ligaments and tendons of the hind limbs are still fairly elastic, which makes it easier to adapt them very progressively to the extreme flexion of the hind joints required for the correct execution of some Grand Prix movements.

The consequences of negligent schooling at this stage are very difficult to reverse. Proof of this is obvious when one sees the number of talented and willing horses in the Grand Prix who are incapable of doing a correct piaffe with ease; the unavailing frantic efforts of the rider transform what should be the most graceful of the High School movements into a ridiculous spectacle. Mere stepping on the spot in diagonals does not conform to the F.E.I. definition of the piaffe, but it has to be said that in this respect the judges frequently bend the rules.

A correct canter pirouette is also impossible if the muscles of a horse's hind limbs are too weak to allow the pronounced flexion of the hocks required by this difficult movement. The rider will have to haul the forehand round with the reins, the turn will be hurried and the rhythm of the canter lost.

The piaffe and the canter pirouette provide the most important indications of accomplished advanced dressage schooling. Denying this shows extraordinary misunderstanding of the purpose of the tests.

The repeated flying changes, including the changes *a tempo*, are (granted that the horse has learnt to understand the rider's intention), more a test of the rider's adroitness than of the horse's athletic prowess. They do not demand particularly pronounced hock flexion; on the contrary, the less the horse is set on the haunches, the more easily can he do the changes. Therefore, there is no particular disadvantage in teaching these movements during the phase of schooling under present discussion. However, a horse who has learnt to develop impulsion in an upward rather than purely forward direction will obviously be better able to shorten his strides and show more spring and elevation in canter.

It is regrettable that, in order to make tests of advanced dressage more difficult, it has been found necessary to multiply the number of required movements. The different aptitudes of horses are not considered. Yet, with very few exceptions, truly great horses are either of the 'campaign' or the 'High School' type and it is unrealistic to expect them to shine equally brilliantly in both the extended movements and the highly collected ones. The rider, therefore, has to accept to some extent the limitations of his horse.

'Campaign' schooling is beneficial for show-jumpers also. A horse who has been physically developed by the practice of gymnastic dressage exercises on the flat is likely to be more successful in stiff competition than an equally talented one who has not received the same sort of training. The show-jumping rider who devotes enough time to the dressage education of his horse will keep his place among the stars more consistently than the one who relies entirely on the natural aptitudes of his partner.

However, advanced dressage schooling of a horse makes much greater demands on a rider's knowledge and ability than 'campaign' training; it requires much more than technical expertise. To train a horse successfully to Grand Prix standard a rider has to be an inspired and consummate artist.

With the exception of the Airs Above the Ground, such as levade, courbette, capriole and so on, all the Airs of the High School are included in the modern Grand Prix. These have kept their names:

piaffe, passage, pirouette, and are defined by the
F.E.I. exactly as they were in the past classical
literature of equitation.

The High School was never just a playful pas-
time for the rich and leisured aristocracy of former
times. It used to be esteemed (though not as much
in England as the rest of Europe) as a serious art,
an edifying spectacle of beauty and grace capable of
developing the aesthetic sensibilities of the public.

In those historical times when an education in
horsemanship and artistic equitation were looked
upon as necessary or desirable accomplishments for
'men of quality', equestrian spectacles were much
appreciated, if only because the rider's apparently
effortless domination of so proud and powerful an
animal as the horse excited wonderment. Yet then,
as nowadays, the spectacle would be appreciated
only if the strength and pride of the horse continued
to be expressed in his eyes and bearing. The sight of
a horse whose spirit has been crushed by insensitive
use of forcible instruments of domination or misconceived methods of training is not enjoyable;
this is the reason why some of the astonishing and
unnatural movements some admittedly very skilful
trainers were able to get a horse to perform incurred
disfavour and have fallen into oblivion. The avowed
purpose of dressage schooling is to refine and perfect
the natural qualities of the horse. When dressage
schooling does violence to nature, it can no longer
be regarded as a decent sport or an art. It degrades
man as much as the horse.

The Airs of the High School have no aesthetic
value if the horse does not appear to perform them
willingly, and I have already explained that this

willingness depends on his ability to execute them easily. They are not difficult for an animal with suitable aptitudes if training has been conducted with intelligence, sympathy and skill but a horse whose understanding and strength have not been sensitively developed by progressive gymnastic exercises will never find them easy. For the judge, ease and willingness are the most important criteria of correct performance of these Airs.

It is an inviolate rule of advanced dressage training that one should never ask for even one step more of piaffe than the horse can execute with ease. Great acquired impulsion is a pre-condition of easy, graceful execution of the piaffe and therefore the rider's aids ought to be so discreet as to be practically invisible. If few horse and rider combinations taking part in dressage competitions at the highest level satisfy these criteria, it must be because the rules of progression have at some time been ignored, with the result that the discomfort associated with execution of the movement remains permanently at the forefront of the horse's memory.

The piaffe is without doubt a most attractive and impressive gait. Sitting to a correct piaffe gives the rider the exhilarating feel of being in control of concentrated forces just about to explode. It follows, therefore, that the piaffe can only be correct if so much impulsion is stored up that the rider's aids need be perceptible only to the horse.

There are horses who seem destined from foalhood for the piaffe. They seem to have a natural loftiness which becomes somewhat suppressed in the first stages of schooling. It is up to the rider to restore during training the horse's appearance of supreme self-confidence, or rather to improve upon what nature has bestowed in the first place.

In a perfectly classical piaffe the horse lowers his haunches by pronouncedly flexing all the hind joints and treading on the spot with greatly engaged hind hooves. The forehand is thus so lightened that each forearm in turn can be held almost at the horizontal for a distinct moment and be lowered without haste. Despite the elevation of the neck, the nose drops towards the vertical, thus enhancing even more the proud appearance of the animal. The toe of the suspended hind limb must not be lifted above the level of the fetlock of the grounded hind foot. Were it lifted higher, either the croup would have to be hitched up or the hock of the suspended limb would just be lifted up instead of advancing under the body. Consequently the hindquarters would be unable to support the major proportion of the weight and the movement would degenerate into what can be best described as a walk in diagonals on the spot in horizontal equilibrium.

When observed, this fault is usually the consequence of methods of training that produce too much flexion of the suspended hock. This exaggerated flexion certainly makes the horse's task easier, since it enables him to evade the inconvenient obligation of supporting weight on a hind limb flexed at all the joints. Once he has discovered this way of avoiding difficulty, the horse will always have recourse to it and will countermand his rider's ever more urgent aids by lifting the croup even more and increasingly sticking to the ground with his forefeet.

The transition from piaffe to passage is one of the

most difficult lessons of the High School. While, in the piaffe, impulsion is needed purely to lighten the forehand at the expense of the hindquarters, in the passage enormous impulsion is required as the loaded hind limb has to assume the dual role of supporting the weight and projecting it forward. Tremendous muscular power is needed in the first step of the passage to extend the previously strongly engaged and flexed hock.

The passage is an extremely cadenced trot, in which the supporting diagonal pair has to remain grounded long enough to provide a distinctly noticeable period of suspension for the other. Like the piaffe, it is a movement of impressive elegance.

Considerable engagement of the hind feet is also necessary for the passage, and the hind hooves should not be picked up any more than in the piaffe. If they were lifted up too high, they would inevitably have to be grounded behind the vertical, and forward propulsion would be insufficient.

Hock flexion is not as great in the passage as in the piaffe and horses who are incapable of performing a correct piaffe may be able to do a correct passage.

Tremendous strength is needed to execute a smooth transition from piaffe to passage. It seems therefore rather unreasonable to insist that a horse must always learn the piaffe before the passage. It is much easier for the horse to develop the passage from the walk or the trot and it does not seem to matter much whether the piaffe is taught before the passage or vice versa. In either case it is always the transition from piaffe to passage which causes the major difficulty. A smooth, unhesitating transition from one to the other is the highest possible achievement for the dressage horse or rider.

The canter pirouette is another movement properly of the High School, but the criteria of correct execution are not sufficiently recognized and it is often demanded of horses who are totally unprepared for its difficulty. A horse has to be extremely athletic to be able to spring 'on a saucer' at the rhythm of the canter. If the muscles of his hind limbs are not up to the task, he will hurry the turn, ground the inside hind too soon, use the rider's hands to preserve his balance, and have to be hauled around by the reins.

The whole purpose of schooling, from the earliest stage, is to strengthen the muscles of the hind limbs. It is a very gradual process, as we have seen, and it must continue without interruption throughout the entire schooling until, in the ultimate stage of the High School, extreme flexion of hocks becomes possible and does not provoke resistance or evasion.

The readiness of the muscles of the hind legs for this exacting Air can be assessed during training by the attitude of the horse in canter voltes and canter half-pass and there is thus no excuse for forcing a horse to execute the canter pirouette before he is quite fit to do so without difficulty. Yet riders in general continue to ignore the criteria for correct execution of this movement, and thoroughly faulty pirouettes are common in performances at High School level.

A canter pirouette is correct if the horse stays perfectly light in the hand, maintains the canter throughout and remains perfectly poised during the execution of the movement, moreover this must be so animated by impulsion that the horse can immediately and fluently resume a light and lively canter on the straight when the rider decides at any moment to stop the pirouette. Impulsion must always remain the most important consideration during the whole time of the horse's education in the canter pirouette but it is impulsion directed more upwards than forwards, and it must therefore come exclusively from the hind legs.

As a result of the development of muscles of the hind legs, the horse is now able to move at all gaits in perfect self-carriage, without the slightest assistance from the reins.

The belief that by leaning backwards the rider assists the horse in the execution of the pirouette is wrong. Extreme 'bracing of the small of the back' makes the rider very stiff and concentrates his weight on the two rear points of his base of support. This compresses intolerably the joints of the horse's hindquarters and forces him either to lean on the hand or to break the canter.

Throughout the duration of the pirouette the rider ought to preserve a correct deep vertical seat. He will know that his horse is not ready for the movement if he does not allow him to maintain his vertical posture with ease. This clearly indicates the necessity to practise again all the movements designed to strengthen the muscles of the hind-quarters before asking for even one more pirouette.

In the days when horses were used for armed combat, the canter pirouette had a practical purpose. It is included in modern dressage not just on account of its difficulty but because it is a very graceful movement − when it is properly executed.

The task of furthering a horse's education to the supreme level of the High School can be tedious if one is interested only in winning ribbons, medals and trophies. A really enthusiastic horseman appreciates as very precious every moment when his horse shows that he understands perfectly his rider's intention and takes pleasure in displaying his agility.

Routine repetition of movements required in a test deprive one of the incomparable delight that such moments give. On the contrary, adherence to the principles of dressage, constant consideration for the horse, and sympathetic adjustment of demands according to his capability, will provide the rider with the incomparable pleasure of feeling that he is creating a long-lasting amicable partnership with his horse.

Dressage competitions at top level are supposed to be primarily demonstrations of superior equestrian knowledge and skill. Besides this they must also have spectator appeal. Nowadays, it seems to be considered necessary to ensure as large an entry as possible at every venue, and we are subjected to the sorry sight of a succession of uninspiring or even distasteful performances.

Yet displays of really artistic horsemanship continue to enchant even a technically uninformed public, and the skill of producing dance-like movements from a remarkably powerful animal without effort and with practically invisible aids is as fascinating for sensitive riders of the present as it was for those of the past.

Horsemanship is more than a skill; it is a science as well as an art. The most artistically inspired rider cannot ignore the scientific principles upon which it is founded. Permanent or even temporary oblivion of those principles would reduce riding to the level of a more or less energetic physical exercise.

The Role of the Spanish Riding
School of Vienna

If certain principles, such as those that have guided the training of horses and riders at the Spanish Riding School of Vienna, have remained incontrovertible for centuries, it can only be because their validity has been proven by experience. These principles have been embodied in the *Directives [of 1898] for the training of horses and riders at the Imperial Spanish High-School of Equitation of Vienna.*

These *Directives* were not intended to be more than general guidelines indicating to the rider the right way of conducting his own education and that of his horse through successive stages on the way to the top. However, they were intended to stress that all methods of training horses had to conform to the principles upon which the classical art of horsemanship was founded.

Riders of the Spanish Riding School are made to understand that there is no fundamental difference between the schooling of the 'campaign' horse and the High School horse. The difference is only one of degree of difficulty. As the regulations of 1898 point out, making a clear-cut distinction between the training of the campaign horse and the education of the High School horse is illogical. Even a horse intended for High School work must first be trained to be a useful, versatile all-rounder. He has to become supple and unresisting in his poll, mouth and back. No specialization can be contemplated before those requirements are fulfilled. There is no reason why natural movement should be ungainly, or artistic movement contrived.

An additional intention of the *Directives* was to prune out superficial refinements and generally simplify and elucidate notions that had become garbled over the years by unrecorded verbal transmission of experience. It was hoped that they would stimulate a renewed interest in High School riding and promote better understanding of an art based on irrefutable scientific principles as well as a long tradition of experience.

However, they firmly asserted that the art of horsemanship was not exclusively the preserve of the High School; the training had to be divided into three stages:

1) Elementary schooling that had to teach the newly backed horse to move calmly, actively and regularly on straight lines, in a form as natural as practical, in the three uncollected gaits of walk, trot and canter.
2) Campaign schooling, during which time the horse had to learn to go on the bit in a collected form, in perfect horizontal equilibrium, at all three gaits, on voltes, turns on the haunches and on two tracks.
3) Training for the High School, when the animal would be required to move with elegant elevation of the forehand, to flex his fully engaged hocks pronouncedly, and to perform in total self-carriage, with great suppleness and agility, the supreme yet never totally artificial Airs of the High School or the Airs Above the Ground.

The now written rule was that the education of all horses had to be conducted according to the same general principle; that the education of all horses had to be progressive; and only horses with outstanding aptitudes for the High School would be required to continue their education through all three stages.

The first stage was not to be considered only as a requirement for horses who showed aptitudes for a more sophisticated education. It applied to all horses regardless of their future utilization. The second stage had to be based on fulfilment of the requirements of the first stage. Schooling in the third stage was not to start before the horse had undergone thorough training through the first two stages and satisfied all the requirements of the military campaign school.

The campaign school was particularly designed to develop impulsion, to improve on the horse's natural carriage and gait, to strengthen the hind limbs and increase the elasticity of the muscles, ligaments, tendons and joints. As a result, the horse would gain in agility and endurance, and his understanding and intelligence would develop. As for the rider, he had to be capable of assessing accurately the mental and physical aptitudes of the horse and of selecting the method of training which he thought most suitable in each particular case. Training a campaign horse was to be an obligatory preparation for the training of a High School horse. The latter had to be considered as the culmination of the education of rider and horse through the two first stages.

The *Directives* also stressed that it was only after satisfactory completion of the first stage that the horse could be deemed sufficiently strong to start learning to move actively with shortened steps in two-track work, showing relative elevation of the forehand, increasing engagement of the hindquarters and flexibility of the hocks; he would also have to be trained to extend himself powerfully in the fast gaits. The principal object of the school had to be the production of useful, enduring and versatile military campaign horses.

Every student at the school would have to undergo as progressive a riding education as the horse's training, and had to be capable of assessing at each stage the state of preparedness of the horse in his charge. He would also have to learn to express succinctly and clearly his estimation of the horse's progress and to explain his plan of training. To put it in a nutshell, the student had to learn not only to ride but also to think, since an unthinking rider will always remain incapable of training a campaign horse within a reasonably short period of time without detriment to soundness and disposition.

Some traditional method and training accessories of the High School continued to be employed at the school. Lungeing in side-reins, for example, was always considered an essential way of introducing a young horse to the habit of working, of teaching him to stretch the reins evenly and of developing the regularity of the trot. Pillars were used to prepare the horse for the Airs of the High School and flexions at the halt were employed to develop the suppleness of the poll. Great importance was attached to the shoulder-in as an ideal way of teaching the rider to coordinate the aids of seat, legs and reins.

The *Directives* also classified the gaits in terms not heard nowadays: there were said to be ordinary gaits, supra-ordinary gaits and artistic gaits. The ordinary gaits were the walk, trot and canter as employed by the unridden, untrained horse at pasture for normal locomotion. The supra-ordinary gaits were the natural passage of the excited horse; turns, springs, short turns, pirouettes, levades, courbettes, ballotades, caprioles and all movements conceived natural when horses play or fight in their wild state. The last four were elaborated into the Airs Above the Ground. The artistic (or sophisticated) gaits were the gaits of the educated horse, collected gaits which the animal would never employ of his own accord in an untamed state: they included the school walk, the school trot, the school canter, the piaffe, the two-track movements and the counter-canter.

The students or *Bereiters* of the school were responsible for the education of individual horses; The *Oberbereiter* (or Riding Master) had the responsibility of organizing quadrilles to music for the entertainment of the nobility and the imperial court. However, the school always strongly deprecated extraordinary equine acrobatics that smacked of vulgar circus showmanship.

The school has always claimed that its methods are derived from the experience and reflections of the great horsemen of the past. The Greek Xenophon is often quoted. He wrote that school riding is not an end in itself, but a means to an end. In other words, no method of schooling is justifiable if it produces a horse unsuitable for military purposes or the chase of wild animals.

Let us hope that the Spanish Riding School of Vienna will continue to demonstrate the close relation of High School riding to 'campaign riding'.